Sarai

Sarai

Is She the Goddess of Ancient Israel?

Dvora Lederman-Daniely

WIPF & STOCK · Eugene, Oregon

SARAI
Is She the Goddess of Ancient Israel?

Copyright © 2021 Dvora Lederman-Daniely. All rights reserved. Except for brief quotations in critical publications or reviews, no part of this book may be reproduced in any manner without prior written permission from the publisher. Write: Permissions, Wipf and Stock Publishers, 199 W. 8th Ave., Suite 3, Eugene, OR 97401.

Wipf & Stock
An Imprint of Wipf and Stock Publishers
199 W. 8th Ave., Suite 3
Eugene, OR 97401

www.wipfandstock.com

PAPERBACK ISBN: 978-1-7252-9888-0
HARDCOVER ISBN: 978-1-7252-9889-7
EBOOK ISBN: 978-1-7252-9890-3

06/25/21

Contents

Introduction: Did Yahweh Have a Consort-Wife? | 1

Chapter 1: The Biblical Story Of Sarai Containing Mythological Fragments | 6

Chapter 2: Canaanite Narratives and their Link with the Narrative in Genesis 12, 18 and 20 | 11

Chapter 3: Sarai as the Name of Asherah | 18

Chapter 4: Could Sarai—Meaning "she who rules"— Be the Name of Asherah? | 20

Chapter 5: Biblical References Portraying a Figure Called Sarai as a Superhuman Being | 23

Chapter 6: The Deir 'Alla Archaeological Discoveries: Evidence of a Goddess Named Sarai? | 36

Chapter 7: The Motif of the Jealous and Punitive Husband in the Bible: Literary Metaphor or Mythical Source? | 40

Chapter 8: Violent Partnering and Parenting: Yahweh's Relationship with His Consort and His Children | 43

Chapter 9: The Mythological Version of the Binding of Isaac | 46

Chapter 10: El Shaddai as El Sarai? | 49

Chapter 11: Has the Name "Sarai" Indicating the Name of the Mother Goddess been Eradicated from the Religion of Israel? | 55

Bibliography | 63

Introduction

Did Yahweh Have a Consort-Wife?

JUDAISM IS A FAITH that sanctifies the male God Yahweh who is characterized by His masculinity. Yahweh is the jealous father, the Lord of hosts, the bridegroom of His metaphorical consort Israel, Jerusalem or Zion. A reading of the scriptures shows, however, that despite this focus on male characteristics, Yahweh is never explicitly portrayed as a God who has a consort—a wife. As such, the portrait of Yahweh as God in partnership with his Goddess wife is an untold story. There is no doubt that biblical religion portrays Yahweh as monotheistic. He has no divine spouse and this negates the legitimate stories told within the Bible itself about the many gods worshipped by the polytheistic religions of the area.

However, critical study of the ancient Israelite religion has shown that despite the monotheistic presentation in the Bible and the interpretations of sages, commentators and translators, the ancient religion of Israel did include a Goddess. This Goddess was Asherah, and She is mentioned in several passages and books of the Bible: Judg 3:7 tells us: "The Israelites did what was offensive to the Lord; they ignored the Lord their God and worshiped the Baalim and the Asheroth." In 2 Kgs 17:16 we read: "They rejected all the commandments of the Lord their God; they made molten idols for themselves—two calves—and they made Ashera and they bowed down to all the host of heaven, and they worshiped Baal."

Sarai

Moreover, 2 Kgs 23:7 states: "He tore down the cubicles of the male prostitutes in the House of the Lord, at the place where the women wove coverings for Asherah."

Scholars have deliberated whether this biblical Asherah is a ritual object—such as a living tree, wooden figure or a forested place of worship—or whether indeed Asherah is the name of a Goddess. Ahituv,[1] for example, believes Asherah was a ritual object. He bases this theory on the term "asherim," which were sacred ritual objects, the biblical prohibition to plant an asherah, and the commandment to cut off the asherah (for example in Exod 34:13). Ahituv claims these references prove Asherah is a ritual object or a tree used for worship, not a divine entity. In contrast, Olyan,[2] Gilula,[3] and Ackerman[4] are among those scholars who maintain that Asherah is definitely a divine entity, and even if in some places she appears as a ritual object, the object represents the Goddess.[5] These biblical scholars stress that this Goddess was a legitimate part of the cult of Yahweh.

Day[6] who also supports this view, bases his claim on studies relating to Ugaritic writings where Athirat appears as the spouse of El. Day explains that Yahweh absorbed the image of El and the relationship with the Goddess—the mother of the gods, who became Asherah, the mother of the children of Israel.

Although biblical authors cast worship of this divine spouse as idolatry, leading to sin, this was in fact contrary to the prevalent cultic religion in the early days of Israel. This portrayal was intended to preserve the appearance of monotheism. It suited the spirit of religious reform that prevailed in the days of Josiah,

---

1. Ahituv, "Asherah in the Bible," 331–36.
2. Olyan, *Asherah and the Cult*, 21.
3. Gilula, "To the Lord of Shomron," 129–37.
4. Ackerman, "Queen Mother," 179–95; Ackerman, "Asherah, the West Semitic Goddess," 1–30.
5. See discussion in Dever, "Archeology and the Ancient Israelite Cult," 9–15.
6. Day, *Yahweh and the Gods and Goddesses*, 42–68. Day, "Asherah in the Hebrew Bible," 385–408.

Did Yahweh Have a Consort-Wife?

which abolished all divinities other than Yahweh. This monotheistic outlook took central place in the edited version of the Bible. Essentially, biblical editors presented a new, more stringent cult in which monotheism was present from the beginning of time, when in fact it was not.[7]

The researchers' claims that Asherah was Yahweh's wife are supported by archaeological discoveries at Kuntillet Ajrud[8] and Khirbat el-Qom[9], which include inscriptions that bless the believer in the name of Yahweh and his Asherah. The Kuntillet Ajrud inscriptions also include frescoes of a crowned bull and a cow accompanied by a female figure playing a harp.[10] Some researchers claim these paintings are linked to the inscriptions and represent Asherah and Yahweh whereas others reject this theory.[11] In any event, archaeological research traces a clear relationship between Yahweh and Asherah.

This literary and religious attempt to obliterate the Goddess, was not entirely successful: within the Bible the shadow of Asherah as a divine spouse remains although veiled in various literary guises. Hadley[12] claims that Bina (Wisdom) in the Book of Proverbs is actually the literary transformation of Asherah. Thus both Lang[13] and Ackerman[14] regard the figure of the Woman of Valor (Eshet Chayil), as she is portrayed in Proverbs 8, as representing the ancient deleted image of Asherah.

Another example of Asherah's transformation in the ancient religion of Israel is the relationship between God and his bride or

---

7. Bin-Nun, "A Brief History," 25–121.
8. Meshel et al., *To the Lord of Teman and Ashera*, 1–35.
9. Dever, "Iron Age Epigraphic Material," 139–204, 165–67.
10. The figure that provides musical accompaniment for the god and his goddess can be found, for example, in Ugaritic mythology, see Cross, *Canaanite Myth and Hebrew Epic*, 21.
11. See discussion in Dever, "Archaeology and the Ancient Israelite Cult," 9–15.
12. Hadley, "From Goddess to Literary Construct," 395–99.
13. Lang, *Wisdom and the Book of Proverbs,* 53–60.
14. Ackerman, "Asherah, the West Semitic Goddess," 1–30.

spouse alternately named as Jerusalem, Zion or Bat Zion. Coogan[15] claims the source of this conjugal metaphor is the divine intimacy between Yahweh and his spouse in ancient Israel's religion.

If so, Coogan is amongst scholars who hypothesize that although the image of Asherah was camouflaged She was preserved in other forms and metaphorically. Passages where the Goddess is represented as God's consort, as written in adjacent religions, were deleted by ancient biblical authors. It is reasonable to assume as is common in the cultures of the region, that the culture and ancient religion of Israel included mythological stories whose heroes were the founding gods—Yahweh and Asherah. But not only do the Genesis stories not explicitly mention Asherah, any shadow of this divine spouse in the Genesis story has largely escaped study by researchers. Indeed, those descriptions in the Book of Genesis that actually merit study as mythological content, are mainly interpreted as controversy. Research has not explored the possibility that canonical texts in Genesis contain remnants or incarnations of an ancient story portraying Yahweh and Asherah as a romantic couple.

In this book, I present the possibility that vestiges of ancient mythology that relate the story of Yahweh's relationship with his spouse, were preserved and interwoven with the stories of Abram and Sarai in the book of Genesis. I will trace enigmatic passages in the story of Sarai, the first mother of Israel. I propose that these passages are stories that depict a divine rather than a human couple, and the consorts are not Abram and Sarai but Sarai and Yahweh. I will show the Ugaritic-Canaanite origins of these narratives and will locate other places in the literary genre of biblical texts that may indicate the divine nature of the female figure called Sarai. This figure was not Abraham's wife, but the similarity of her name, and the fact that she was established as an early mother of Israel, together with the fact that the authors and later editors of the Bible did not seem to recognize this ancient divine figure, probably accounts for her figure being merged with the human figure of Sarai/Sarah, the wife of Abraham.

---

15. Coogan, "Canaanite Origins and Lineage," 119–20.

Did Yahweh Have a Consort-Wife?

The chapters of the book will discuss the mythological plot sections, and the complexity of the relationship they reveal between Yahweh and his consort. This sheds new, unsettling light on the relationship, on its significance, and the origins of the ancient motif of the husband who punishes his treacherous spouse. In the Bible this has been presented as the people's betrayal of their God and their punishment for idolatry.

I will also show how the assumption that Sarai was the name of an ancient Goddess is integrated into and supported by archaeological evidence concerning an ancient deity, that has been lost and immersed in the dust of the historical memory of ancient Israel.

Chapter 1

The Biblical Story Of Sarai Containing Mythological Fragments

SARAH IS THE FIRST mother of the Hebrew nation. She is notable mainly because she is barren. We are told that Abraham takes her as his wife, and she accompanies him on his mission to fulfil his destiny. She is not a partner, at least not explicitly, to the injunction to Go Forth (Lech Lecha) addressed to Abraham. Sarah, alternatively spelled Sarai in the Bible, is not called upon to withstand mighty tests of faith as is Abraham, nor does she share the Covenant with God or the promise of the land given directly to Abraham.[1] She receives the blessing indirectly through the pledge to Abraham's seed, which is also the intended fruit of her womb.[2]

---

1. In connection with Sarah's involvement and marginality, Yedgar concludes the fact, passed down from generation to generation, that there is no reference to a direct covenant with Sarah, raises the question of whether the matriarchs were considered active partners in the covenant with God. This establishes the severance of the matriarchs of the nation from any spiritual status, in contrast to the patriarchs. See, Yedgar, "Sarah's Words," 46.

2. There is an assumption that the double promise of the birth of an heir in Chapters 17 and 18 arose from the later addition of Chapter 17 to reinforce and emphasize Isaac's spiritual precedence over Ishmael. On the other hand, another argument for the later addition of Chapter 17 is Zakovitch's argument that the emphasis of the promise to Abraham as the father of many nations is intended to prevent an interpretation that only Sarai was crowned as the

The Biblical Story Of Sarai Containing Mythological Fragments

The story of how Abraham offers Sarah/Sarai sexually to foreign kings in order to save his life, while her voice remains unheard, emphasizes her position as a silent, physical object and commodity.[3] Moreover, the conflict she encounters with Hagar, her servant, does not benefit her, since it gives the impression that she is an obsessive and petty wife, especially when compared with Abraham's nobility and generosity.

However, parts of Sarai's story do not logically match her relatively marginal figure, nor her status as Abraham's wife who is supposed to bear his successor. One such part of the story is the dialogue between Sarai and "the Lord" God in Gen 18:12–15. In these passages "the Lord" God asks why Sarai laughed.

This conversation is to a large extent enigmatic. God insists that Sarai laughed, whereas in this volume another meaning for 'laughed' is interpreted. Examined closely, this conversation is not on the level of spiritual guidance, but seems rather to be an everyday conversation between equals.[4] Moreover, there is a strange inaccuracy in God's repetition of Sarah's words.

Sarah asks defiantly whether she can still experience pleasure (in this volume this is interpreted to be sexual pleasure) since her husband is old (Gen 18:12). In response, God answers: "Wherefore did Sarah laugh, saying: Shall I of a surety bear a child? and I am old?"

Sarah speaks of her husband's old age, yet God quotes her words as if she is speaking of her own advanced age. Researchers have interpreted the imprecision and modification expressed by God: Bakon,[5] for example, presents various explanations for this inaccuracy, including Rashi's interpretation that God altered

---

mother of many nations. Zakovitch claims the blessing to Abraham "and I will make nations of thee" (Gen 17:6) that was added later, originates from the blessing to Sarah, "I will bless her, and she shall be a mother of nations" (Gen 17:16). It is possible, as I will later claim, that the description of Sarai as the mother of many nations belongs to the divine Sarai and not necessarily to the earthly Sarai/h. Zakovitch, "Woman in Biblical Stories," 14–32.

3. See on this topic, Van Dijk-Hemmes, "Sarai's Exile," 220–35.
4. See Bakon, "Biblical Dialogues," 397–430.
5. Bakon, "Biblical Dialogues," 400.

Sarai

Sarah's words out of respect for Abraham's honour, so as not to describe him as an old man.

In this study, I raise another possibility based on a reexamination of additional sections of the discourse between God and Sarai, through a comparison with relevant Ugaritic mythology. I suggest that God is actually quoting Sarah's words accurately. In verse 12, after speaking of her doubt that she can conceive, God switches from repeating Sarah's words to speaking in the first person, as he continues to hone her argument. The words "and I am old" are not a direct quote from Sarah, for she did not say it, but rather a switch to first-person speech. So when God repeats what Sarah said about him, he is saying, "You said that I am old." God is identifying Himself as the one whom Sarah describes as her husband.

This theory connecting God and Sarah—that is, He is her husband and She is His spouse—may seem strange, but in fact there are more expressions in the discourse between God and Sarah that may attest to just such a relationship between God and a character named Sarai or Sarah.

In Gen 18:13, when God repeats His promise that Sarah will give birth to a son, she laughs. Strangely, God focuses on her laughter and repeatedly asks—"Wherefore did Sarah laugh?" (18:13). Although we have the impression that the laughter stems from Sarah's lack of faith, the repetition and focus on the word "to laugh" in the accusatory form obliges us to examine the lesser known meanings of the word in this context.[6]

The Book of Genesis uses the word Letzahek לצחק from the root צחק, which means "laugh" in Hebrew, not only in the sense of laughter or mockery, as translated in this context, but also in the flirtatious-romantic sense. In Gen 26 we read: "And behold, Isaac was sporting with Rebekah his wife" (26:8). The English translation uses the word "sporting," but the Hebrew uses מצחק

---

6. A discussion of the various meaning of the verb "tsehok" can be found in Shkop, "Sarah Laughed," 42–51. The interpretations presented are "Orthodox," but the conclusion that—"the root 'tsehok' always implies laughter with a twist, laughter that hides something" (Shkop, "Sarah Laughed," 50) also fits my argument regarding Sarah's laughter, although the "twist" that I propose is far more extreme and revolutionary.

The Biblical Story Of Sarai Containing Mythological Fragments

—"laughing." When King Avimelech hears the laughter between Isaac and Rebekah, he realizes they are lovers and not brother and sister, as Isaac had claimed.

In Gen 39:17 Potiphar's wife uses the word Letzahek לצחק as another term for "lying with me" (39:14). Thus in some cases the Book of Genesis uses the word Letzahek to mean sexual flirtation and seduction.

Based on this meaning of the word "laugh" or צחקה, God's insistence on the fact that Sarah laughed can be linked to the suspicious interrogation of a jealous spouse, involving an accusation of seductive sexual intention or behaviour.

In addition to the verb "to laugh," the description of Sarah as one who denies ("and Sarah denies" Gen 15:15) suggests a serious accusation and a much more severe crisis of trust than is evident at the surface level of the text.

In many places in the Bible people who deny something are sinners against God. In the Book of Joshua we read: "Israel hath sinned; yea, they have even transgressed My covenant which I commanded them; yea, they have even taken of that which is proscribed; and have also stolen, and dissembled" (Josh 7:11). (In the Hebrew version the same word לכחש (Lekahesh) is used in both verses). In Isa 30:9 we read: "For it is a rebellious people, lying children, children that refuse to hear the teaching of the Lord." They ignore God's existence and therefore refuse to hear His teachings. Isaiah says in Chapter 59: "Transgressing and denying the Lord, and turning away from following our God, speaking oppression and perverseness, conceiving and uttering from the heart words of falsehood" (30:13). The same applies in Jer 5:12, Job 31:28, and Prov 30:9: "Lest I be full, and deny, and say: 'Who is the Lord?' Or lest I be poor, and steal, and profane the name of my God."

Those who deny God (מכחשים) are not people upon whose words and loyalty God can rely. This is why the description of Sarai as "denying" (ותכחש) reinforces the hypothesis of a difficult relationship marked by betrayal and mistrust.

The meanings of the words "laugh" (Letzahek לצחק) and "deny" (לכחש Lekahesh) that may attest to an accusation of betrayal of trust as the result of sexual temptation and betrayal do not exist in a vacuum, disconnected from events. We should bear in mind that in Gen 12, Sarah is actually conducting intimate relations with a man who is not her husband. In the scenario where Abraham tells her "Thou are my sister" he tries to save his own life by giving his wife, the mother of his future heir, to a foreign king—to be taken to his palace and perhaps to his bed.[7] The narrator does not relate what happened to Sarai in Pharaoh's palace, but it can be assumed that if the king took her because of her great beauty, and she spent some time in the palace, intimate relations likely ensued.[8] This situation in which a husband gives his wife, the mother of his future heir, to another man, is illogical but it is the first of two such events involving Sarah.

It seems that the plot of "Thou art my sister" is taken from a different context, since it is unlikely that the Patriarch Abraham would jeopardize his sexual ownership of his wife, as well as the certainty of his paternity over Sarai's future son. It has therefore been argued that this event is disconnected from the context of the other stories of Abraham and Sarai.[9]

It is important to note that it is God—not Abraham—who fights for Sarai and saves her. Thus, it is God, not Abraham who expresses jealousy and acts to prevent her betraying him intimately. In other words, here God plays the role of the betrayed husband.

Based on the discussion thus far, we can query whether some sections of Sarai's story, such as "Thou art my sister," and the dialogue with God in Chapter 18, could in fact be referring to narratives other than that of Abraham and Sarai? Is it possible that these sections refer to another couple, mythological in character—God Yahweh and his spouse?

---

7. Many studies have attempted to explain this, see for example, Speiser et al., "Wife-Sister Motif," 62–82.

8. Peleg, "Did Pharaoh Touch Sarai?" 54–64.

9. Aharoni, "Three Similar Stories," 213–23.

Chapter 2

Canaanite Narratives and their Link with the Narrative in Genesis 12, 18 and 20

THE BIBLICAL TEXT IS composed of traditions transmitted over the generations, both orally and in writing. These traditions were influenced by the religions and cultures of the region. Popular oral tales of the ancient Near East shared many similarities[1] and some were actually different versions of the same story. Greenstein,[2] who reveals a parallel between the Mesopotamian and biblical stories, argues that this parallel stems from the influence of these texts on the Hebrew narrator. Talshir[3] also identified the prominent influence of Canaanite and Hittite literature on the biblical narrative. Diverse traditions merged into an apparently uniform text. Considering this it is possible that the saga of Abraham and Sarai incorporated stories from different traditions which were also influenced by the narratives of neighbouring cultures and religions. They may have also combined stories about figures who were perceived as belonging to the saga of Abraham and Sarai for various reasons, including the similarity of their names.

1. Yulzary, "Introduction," 9–29.
2. Greenstein, "From Oral Epic to Written Verse," 47–64.
3. Talshir, *Biblical Literature*, 521.

Sarai

In light of the observation that the discourse described in Gen 18 may in fact be a dialogue between Yahweh and His spouse, in which He suspects sexual flirtation or seduction, and in light of the assumption that 'Thou art my sister" may be detached from the context of the Abraham and Sarai story, it is possible that these narrative fragments are what remains of a mythological tale. This missing mythological narrative describes the story of Yahweh and His spouse and centres on sexual relations between the Goddess and a strange god, and the jealousy that it provoked in her husband.

As is often the case in the study of ancient Israel and the Bible, we can learn about concepts, roles or narratives that were censored in monotheistic editing through the study of the religions of the region that did not undergo such censorship. The assumption that such a mythological story existed in the ancient religion of Israel is reinforced by the existence of a similar story in Ugaritic mythology that heavily influenced the shaping of Yahweh's image.

Day,[4] who studied the relations between Yahweh and other deities in the Canaanite and Mesopotamian regions, noted that the image of the Ugaritic god was absorbed into the image of Yahweh, as was the relationship with the Goddess and some other elements. Day maintains that Yahweh did not come from Canaan. El was the ruling deity in Canaan during the pre-mosaic period, and his attributes were assimilated into Yahweh. Day details these traits, which include: old age, wisdom, responsibility for creation (the Creator of heaven and earth), and fathering his sons. In addition, Day maintains that Yahweh married the Goddess Asherah.

Pope's study,[5] which explored the marital relationship between El and Asherah, revealed a conflict situation that may be relevant to this study. From the Ugaritic text it emerges that El's sexual prowess was inadequate: he does not satisfy Asherah's sexual needs. According to Pope, El must overcome his impotence and to achieve this he performs a magic ritual involving a bird and a staff, apparently hinting at his sexual organ, as his "love staff." In the magic ritual the bird is consumed by fire. Pope maintains

---

4. Day, *Yahweh and the Gods and Goddesses*, 13–42.
5. Pope, *El*, 37.

Canaanite Narratives and their Link with the Narrative

that the staff and the hand are phallic symbols, initially described as drooping and flaccid, but once they have passed through the fire they seem to rise. After the ceremony El kisses his wives and causes them to conceive, from which it can be deduced that he is no longer impotent.[6]

This understanding of the intimate relationship between Asherah and El, according to Pope, accords with the Hittite mythology that features Elkunirsa and Asheratu. In the Hittite mythology the goddess Ashertu tempts the storm god—Baal, and he tells her consort, the god Elkunirsa, about the temptation. The supreme god is furious. He commands Baal to return to this woman, to sleep with her, and to humiliate her by slaughtering her sons.

According to Pope, in light of what is known about the relationship of El and Asherah, and El's impotence, it is understandable that Asheratu (the equivalent Goddess to Asherah) turns to Baal. Unlike the impotent El, Baal is younger, instinctive and virile, and she wants him to fulfil the sexual urges that are not being satisfied by her aged husband.

What is interesting about the Hittite myth and its connection to Ugaritic mythology is the clear connection to the biblical God. Talshir,[7] claims that the names of the gods in the myth of Elkunirsa and Asheratu leave little room for doubt as to their origin: Asheratu is the Canaanite Asherah, and the Hittite Elkunirsa is actually the name of "God Most High, Maker of heaven and earth," as He is being presented in Gen 14:19. In other words, the same divine appellation appears in the story of El and Asheratu as in Genesis.

Apart from identifying the name of God, we can distinguish similar characteristics between the stories in Genesis involving Abraham and Sarai and the Ugaritic-Hittite mythology.

Both in Genesis and in the mythology the characters are described as sitting in a tent, and both of them mention laughter. In the mythological story El laughs as Asherah enters his tent, a laugh of sexual anticipation and enthusiasm. Pope speculates that this is

6. Pope, *El*, 39.
7. Talshir, *Biblical Literature*, 38.

Sarai

due to the improper relations between them and the distancing of Asherah, which is why El is so excited to see her. In the story in Genesis the laughter is attributed to Sarah. In both narratives the laughter is an explosive element.

In both cases, the emphasis is on the advanced age of the husband. In the mythological story a main characteristic of El is his old age. As I maintain, God's old age is referred to in Genesis, since the expression "and I am old," does not in fact refer to Sarah's age, but to God's description of himself, with reference to Sarah's words.

Both cases also mention the sexual dissatisfaction experienced by the female partner because of the age of her spouse. It is clearly presented in the Ugaritic writings studied by Pope, and in Genesis it is portrayed in a more veiled manner.

It was written about Sarah: "And Sarah laughed to herself, saying, 'Now that I am withered, am I to have enjoyment—with my husband so old?'" (Gen 18:12). Indeed, due to the narrator's preliminary remarks that Sarah had ceased to menstruate ("Sarah had stopped having the periods of women" 18:11) the reader accepts her mention of being withered (in Hebrew "bloti," "בלתי") and takes this to mean Sarah is in menopause. Consequently, the pleasure Sarah speaks of is understood in the context of childbirth. However, in Hebrew the root "בלה" relates to a worn-out garment, or shoe: "I led you through the wilderness forty years. The clothes on your back did not wear out (balu בלו) nor did the sandals on your feet" (Deut 29:4). See also Isaiah (50:9): "Lo, the Lord God will help me—Who can get a verdict against me? They shall wear out (יבל) like a garment, the moth shall consume them." Thus it is possible that Sarah compares herself and her worn-out appearance to a worn-out garment, something that is less attractive and less alluring. She is therefore surprised to hear that under these circumstances she will experience pleasure and enjoyment.

Shaviv,[8] notes that the word that Sarah uses—"Edna," (pleasure) "עדנה" is related to a vibrant, physical and instinctive state. The word can also be associated with passionate youthfulness. Sarah is, therefore, making a connection between the fact that

---

8. Shaviv, "עד, עדנה, עדיך," 295–99.

Canaanite Narratives and their Link with the Narrative

she is less attractive and the physical pleasure she will experience. Her remark could imply that she has not experienced sexual pleasure, due to her husband's advanced age and sexual impotence. Thus, according to this interpretation, the marital relationship illustrated in Gen 18 is similar to the marital relationship between Asherah and El that is portrayed in Ugaritic mythology. It should also be noted that in the mythological depiction of the magical ritual performed by El to restore his sexual potency at a time when his "love staff" is described as flaccid, there is no reference to his ability to have an erection after the ceremony. However, we can assume this occurs given the narrative about the women who kiss him and conceive.[9] Conception serves to illustrate the power of manhood. In parallel, the emphasis on Sarah's future conception in the discourse in Chapter 18 and its accompanying pleasure (עדנה) may refer to her future sexual satisfaction.

In both the Ugaritic myth and the biblical story, the theme of the wife's sexual experience with a man who is not her husband can be linked to the sexual dissatisfaction and sexually frustrating relationship that she has with her husband. Thus, the mythological Hittite story of Elkunirsa and Asheratu in which she attempts to seduce Baal, becomes understandable in the light of the sexual frustration revealed in the Ugaritic writings. In parallel, the "Thou art my sister" event in Gen 12, where Sarah is sexually available to a man who is not her husband, can be understood in a different way from that portrayed, given her sexual frustration with her husband, as implied in Gen 18.

If we also relate to the second "Thou are my sister" scene, which takes place with Avimelech the King of Gerar, this may depict the pleasure Sarai speaks of in Chapter 18. Although the narrator emphasizes that Avimelech did not touch Sarai, nevertheless, based on the Hebrew correlation between "touch" (נגע naga) and "plagues" (נגעים negaim), that appears in Gen 12, this is a case of 'quid pro quo'—because Pharaoh touched (נגע) Sarai, Egypt was smitten by plagues (נגעים).[10] The punishment casually referred to

---

9. Pope, *El*, 40–41.
10. See Yavin, *Queen*, 73–78.

at the end of the scene with Avimelech, according to which God closed up the wombs of the women in Avimelech's kingdom, may actually serve as an indication of a component that may have been blurred or censored in the edited version. In the sense of "measure for measure" the women's wombs were "obstructed," perhaps because Avimelech "released the obstruction" in Sarai's womb. The narrator goes out of his way to assure his readers that the predictable did not happen—Avimelech did not approach Sarah, but She returns pregnant from his house, for indeed the following verse reads: 'And the Lord came to Sarah . . . Sarah conceived and gave birth . . . ' (Gen 21:12). If we connect conception with pleasure or with the husband's sexual prowess, as claimed above, then Sarah did experience the pleasure she anticipated in Gen 18.

In light of the striking similarity between the Ugaritic and the biblical narratives, it may be that Gen Chapters 12, 18 and 20 are vestiges of an ancient Israelite mythology rooted in Ugaritic and Hittite myth, or that both stories share a common origin. These passages concern God and His spouse, and the temptations and jealousy entailed in their relationship. The full stories have probably been lost. They perhaps vanished in the course of time, as the Israelite religion developed, or they were erased during the editing of the Book of Genesis. It is likely though that prominent and salacious remnants of these stories were somehow preserved and compounded with the story of Sarah and Abraham. This merging may have resulted from the similarity between the human Sarah/Sarai's name and the name of the Goddess Asherah or Asheratu. It is possible that this similarity led to the integration of that story into the tradition of the Abraham and Sarai narrative. Another possibility is that this is not about the similarity in names but about the identity of the name that led to a merging of these sections in the story of Sarai and Abraham. In other words, it is possible that Sarai was the epithet of the Hebrew Goddess, the divine spouse, who is alluded to in the critical study of the ancient religion of Israel.

It is possible that the early biblical editor was unaware of the name of the ancient Goddess because her name had been lost over time. The editor therefore associated the Goddess's name with the mortal Sarai who was Abraham's wife. A further possibility is that the editor was familiar with the name of this female deity, but for ideological reasons he believed it was a forbidden name in the religion of Israel. The editor might then have taken it upon himself to erase this forbidden past in the book dedicated to the founding of the nation. Thus the image of the divine spouse, Sarai, merged with that of a human spouse, Sarah. It is possible that Gen 17 story of how the name was changed from Sarai to Sarah is a "cover story" intended to explain why the character of Sarai has two names. To show that not only Sarai's name was changed, we are also told that Abraham's name was also changed.[11]

---

11. Fleishman, "On the Significance of a Name Change," 310–21; Sutskover, "Name Giving in Genesis," 33–51; Sutskover claims the name change was based on a relationship of control and ownership, when Abraham is depicted as calling Sarai by her new name, Sarah, this demonstrates his mastery over her.

Chapter 3

Sarai as the Name of Asherah

AT THIS STAGE THERE is an obvious question and it is this: Is it possible that Sarai was an epithet of the Goddess Asherah, the spouse of Yahweh?

To answer this question, we must first note that the sound and graphic combination of the letters šr that characterize Sarai's name is typical of the mother goddesses in the local religions. The combination of the letters "šr" or "שר" appears in the names of the following goddesses: the Canaanite Ašerah, the Babylonian Ašartum, Phoenician Ašeratu and Akkadian Aširtu, or Ašratum who was also called šarat.

The combination "širu" symbolized sanctity or the Temple itself. It is the equivalent of the Akkadian word "Elu," i.e., the equivalent of the name of the male god. Hence the names of the mother-goddesses, combined with šr, were an indication of their sanctity and their superior divine position. We can therefore assume that the name of the divine spouse in the mythological Israelite narrative could have included the šr combination.

Secondly, it should be noted that the suffix "ai" existed in ancient western Semitic languages, and appears in the names of Canaanite female deities such as Tallai, and Arsai.[1] In the Bible, this feminine suffix appears only in the name of Sarai, thus

---

1. Layton, *Archaic Features*, 28, 244–48.

Sarai as the Name of Asherah

strengthening the argument that Sarai was the ancient epithet of a female deity that was changed at a later stage to avoid identifying it with the divinity. Alternatively, this feminine construction may have ceased to exist.

In the Canaanite language, the suffix "ai" served to denote "the one responsible for a particular phenomenon."[2] Accordingly, if we examine the root of Sarai's name to ascertain the particular phenomenon or quality associated with it, based on this Canaanite principal, the name Sarai can mean "she who rules."

The meaning of the word Šarat or Šarratu in Mesopotamian languages is "queen." The name of Sennacherib's wife, according to writings from the 6th century BCE, was Tasmetum Šarrat. Mar Šarri was the name of the crown prince. From the Bible we learn that the "שר" , sr combination means "to rule," "to govern," "to have authority." It indicates high social rank. Similarly, the biblical expression "שרי כוהנים" Sarei kohanim" or "chiefs of the priests" is used to describe those who hold senior religious positions and indicates a superior status. See for example, Ezra 10:5: "Then arose Ezra, and made the chiefs of the priests . . ." In other words, the use of the šr/sr root denotes kingship, high ranking and governance. In early writings the letter Š (sh) appears, but in the Bible the Š becomes S, and shr becomes sr, for example, "*sh*arei cohanim" became "*s*arrei cohanim" (Ezra 10:5). In Hebrew the same letter is used but with different punctuation. Since punctuation was added at a later stage, this may be the source of the change, so Sarai could at an earlier stage have been Šarai. Thus based on this, Sarai could be an ancient epithet for a female deity who is perceived to be a divine queen.

---

2. Lutzky, "Shadday," 17–18.

Chapter 4

Could Sarai—Meaning "she who rules"—Be the Name of Asherah?

GIVEN THE NAME SARAI means "she who rules," and that this book's thesis is that Sarai was the epithet for Asherah, can the argument be taken further to show this Goddess was a ruling goddess and therefore was a queen?

As discussed in earlier chapters, the image of Ugaritic El greatly influenced the image of Yahweh, as well as his relationship with his wife, Asherah. If we look at the status of El and Asherah as revealed in the Ugaritic texts of Ras Shamra, it was certainly that of a king and a queen. El and Asherah were the heads of a divine council with a clear hierarchy. They stood at its head, and the rest of the gods were their entourage.[1] The ranks of the gods are presented as a royal bureaucracy (along the lines of a family system). El is described as mlk ab snm,[2] Lord of the Heavens and Most High. He functions as the ruler who decides destinies and makes decisions.[3]

---

1. Greenstein, "Canaanite Pantheon," 55; Rendtorff, "The Background," 167–70.
2. Pope, *El*, 25.
3. Greenstein, "Canaanite Pantheon," 55.

Could Sarai—Meaning "she who rules"—Be the Name of Asherah?

Yahweh, who assimilated El's attributes, is also described with the status of a ruling king. Judg 8: 22-23 says: "And Gideon said to them, I will not rule over you, and my son will not rule over you, the Lord will rule over you." In other words, the concept is that Yahweh is the only ruler—the only king. God is depicted as accompanied by subordinate gods and His entourage is described as "ten thousand holy ones" (Deut 33:2). In the Song of Deborah (Judg 5) the stars, God's entourage, descend from their orbits to help God in His war.[4] These descriptions are very similar to descriptions of the Divine Council in Ugaritic literature, and the status of the Lord corresponds to the status of the Ugaritic El, king of the gods.

Taking this argument further, Yahweh's kingdom is described as a roaring lion cub—"And the Lord will roar from Zion, and shout aloud from Jerusalem" (Joel 4:16). The lion represents royal status in the ancient East,[5] but not only was this the symbol of the male God, but it also featured prominently in archeological evidence where it is the symbol of the Goddess.

Indeed, the most prominent reference to Ashera is as the mother of the gods, that is, the emphasis is usually on the family aspect and her maternal role. But there are other aspects to Asherah. Her image, as reflected in reliefs and paintings, is depicted as standing above lions. From the Late Bronze Age, her most prominent iconographic appearance is as the "naked goddess" standing above the lion. In other words, she rules the lion and is carried by him.[6]

In the late 9th/early 8th century archaeological findings at Kuntillet Ajrud, the female divine figure is replaced by the symbol of the tree and the ibex, Asherah's iconographic symbol. The ibexes and the tree are drawn above the lion, next to the inscription—"Yahweh and his Asherah."[7] Thus Asherah is symbolized by the status symbol of the kingship—the lion.

4. Cross, *Canaanite Myth and Hebrew Epic*, 70-105.
5. Keel and Uehlinger, *Gods, Goddesses and Images of God*, 19; Ornan et al., "'Lord will Roar from Zion,'" 1-13, 269.
6. Ornan, "Gods and Symbols," 70, 82.
7. Hadley, *Cult* of *Asherah*, 84-100.

Sarai

Apart from iconographic symbols, in Ugaritic mythology Asherah is portrayed as a queen alongside El. Although she is dependent on his decisions, as his queen, she governs the other gods, and they, like Baal, turn to her to influence El's decisions.

Beyond these findings, evidence in the Bible itself indicates Asherah's position as a ruling queen. Jer 7: 16–19, for example uses the term "Queen of Heaven," which according to some scholars represents Asherah and captures her queenly status.[8] This goddess-queen is described as being venerated by the people of Judea, who bring her incense and offerings. According to Jeremiah, the Judean women would prepare cakes in her image, and the whole family partook of this ritual. The belief was that these rituals would lead to a good life, security and abundance. Koch[9] who associates the Queen of Heaven with Asherah, relies, among other things, on 2 Kgs 22:4, 5–6:

> Then the king ordered the high priest Hilkiah, the priests of the second rank, and the guards of the threshold to bring out of the Temple of the Lord all the objects made for Baal and Asherah and all the host of heaven. He burned them outside Jerusalem ... And those who made offerings to Baal, to the sun and moon and constellations—all the host of heaven. He brought out the Asherah from the House of the Lord to the Kidron Valley outside Jerusalem, and burned it in the Kidron Valley.

These verses make a clear connection between the worship of celestial astral beings and Asherah. The army of the heavens, which includes the sun, the moon and the stars, is mentioned in the context of Asherah's ritual objects. Thus she may well be called the Queen of Heaven, the one in charge of the heavenly army.

From the discussion in this chapter it is clear that "she who rules" may well be a reference to Asherah.

---

8. See discussion in Hadley, "Queen of Heaven," 30–54; Ackerman, "'And the Women Knead Dough,'" 21–33.

9. Koch, "Aschera als Himmelskönigin," 97–120.

Chapter 5

Biblical References Portraying a Figure Called Sarai as a Superhuman Being

BEYOND EXPLORING THE DISCOURSE of Sarai in the context of Genesis narratives and the saga of Abraham and Sarai, further evidence, perhaps ancient textual remnants, can be found for the superhuman and mythological character of a female figure called Sarai in the religion of Israel.

"Sarati" in the Book of Lamentations

Lamentations 1:1 reads: "How doth the city sit solitary that was full of people! How is she become as a widow! She that was great ('*Raba*ti' 'רבתי' in Hebrew), among the nations, and princess ('*Sara*ti' 'שרתי' in Hebrew,) among the provinces, how is she become a tributary!" The addition of 'ti' as it appears in the verse is a grammatical construct indicating possession—"my Sarai."
    This verse in the Hebrew reveals a parallel between the word "Sarai" and the name "Raba." "Raba" or rbt meaning the Great One[1] was the epithet of the Goddess, in the neighbouring cultures.

---

1. Avinery, "Position," 123–27.

Sarai

In the relevant context, "Raba" or rbt was Asherah's epithet.[2] Raba Athirat was the name used for Asherah.

The clear interpretation of verse 1 of Lamentations is that the words *sarati* and *rabati* describe Jerusalem as a ruined city, in the sense of the ruined kingdom of Judea and the destroyed Temple. The ruined city assumes the qualities of a feminine entity, Bat Zion, described as betrayed, weeping, exposed, impure, and dejected. The kingdom that was exalted and sublime has lost everything. She is rejected and she is wretched.

However, if "Sarai" in its various forms was the name of the ancient Hebrew Goddess, then the mention of her name *sarati* coupled with *rabati* (the great one) at the beginning of the first chapter may have originally indicated that this was a lamentation of the Goddess. Alternatively, it could have been the lamentation of the author and the people for the destruction, the distress, or the contempt suffered by the Goddess. Sarai, the mother Goddess of the people of Israel, weeps and laments, and it is not only the anthropomorphized figure of Jerusalem that is mourning, not only Jerusalem that is described as trampled, but also the Goddess who was worshiped in Jerusalem. She has also fallen from power. She has been humiliated and trampled. We know that Bible records show the Temple contained objects of worship and symbols of Ashera alongside those of Yahweh. As the people are exiled from their country, so too are they exiled from their mother Goddess.

Support for this ancient meaning of the lamentation can be found in several descriptions given by the composer of the Book of Lamentations. First, Lamentations verse 6 mentions one of the prominent religious symbols of Asherah, as mentioned earlier. This is the tree and ibex, which was the symbol of abundance, fertility, and divine nourishment:[3] "Gone from Zion are all that were her glory; her leaders were like deer that found no pasture; they could only walk feebly before their pursuer" (Lamentations 1:6). In the author's description, the deer/ibex did not find a place

---

2. Cornelius, *Many Faces*, 99.

3. Keel and Uehlinger, *Gods, Goddesses and Images of God,* 26, 147–49; Ornan, "Gods and Symbols," 70, 82.

Biblical References Portraying a Figure Called Sarai

to feed. The iconographic icon for abundance and nourishment is severely breached. The Goddess can no longer provide security, nourishment and abundance, and the prevailing condition is one of deficiency, distress and suffering. The canonical author probably was not referring to the Goddess herself when he used her symbol, but the earlier version of the lament may have dealt with the Goddess by using her accepted symbols. Later, due to the changes in Israel's religion and the process of biblical editing, the symbol remained as a poetic literary image, without the editor's awareness of its original significance.

Further support for the divine nature of the feminine entity known as "Sarati" in Lamentations 1:1 can be found in the interpretation scholars have given to the ancient meaning of "Bat Zion," which is another important appellation. Dobbs-Alsopp[4] claims the source of the amalgamation of Bat Zion in the Book of Lamentations is the Mesopotamian figure of the lamenting goddess. The biblical lament, it is argued, was heavily influenced by the Mesopotamian lamentation. Klein[5] sees in the Book of Lamentations a marked similarity to Mesopotamian lamentations where the female entity is the Goddess who laments her city, her shrine, and her ruined kingdom. In these laments, the author's description of the goddess mourning the destruction is intertwined with the direct plea and cry of the goddess herself. The author typically encourages the goddess to lament and cry to the supreme god who is responsible for the destruction, and sometimes the people lament their city and their Goddess.[6]

For example, in the Mesopotamian lamentation for the city of Ur, the words of the goddess Ningal, wife of the patron god of the city, are heard.[7] The speakers are the narrator and the Goddess:

"The lady/daughter in her house which was plundered,
for which she weeps bitterly,

---

4. Dobbs-Allsopp, "Syntagma of Bat," 467–70.
5. Klein, "Bat-Ṣiyon," 177–207.
6. Klein, "Bat-Ṣiyon," 198–99.
7. There is a marked similarity between these lines and Lam 1:11–22, and Lam 2:18–22.

> Nana whose land is lost,
> The light of his people will lament, the faithful woman, the lady will sigh for her city
> Nangal—for the sake of not giving respite to her eyelids for her land
> Light, for the sake of her city, she will sacrifice, she will weep bitterly
> For her home, which he robbed, the lady will sacrifice, she will cry bitterly...[8]

The characteristics of the Mesopotamian lamentation also appear in the Book of Lamentations, in which the female entity of Bat Zion or Jerusalem mourns the destruction, and there is an interaction between the author's voice and her own lament or that of her people.

In Mesopotamian literature the lamenting Goddess is frequently referred to as "Bat"—"daughter" (märat) in conjunction with the name of the ruined city. For example, in the Babylonian lament of Tammuz, Ishtar is called "Bat Nopur" when she laments her husband and her city [9] (märat Larak or märat Nippuri).

The juxtaposition that included the word "bat" and the city name, indicates the name for the patron Goddess of the city. Klein did not mean, however, that the author of the Scroll was lamenting the Goddess, maintaining that it was merely a borrowed literary image. But Fitzgerald,[10] points out that in Israelite-Canaanite circles it could have been the Goddess lamenting.

It is interesting to learn from this about the ancient parallel between the name of the city and the name of the Goddess who is considered to be its patron. It may be that the Goddess, Yahweh's consort, was seen as a patron of Zion or Jerusalem. Therefore, the names Zion or Jerusalem were common names for the Goddess herself.

Hence when Isaiah (66:8–9) speaks of Zion who gave birth to the people of Israel, in the sense of supernatural creation-birth,

---

8. Shifra and Klein, *In those Distant Days*, 42.
9. Klein, "Bat-Ṣiyon," 203.
10. Fitzgerald, "Mythological Background," 37, 403–16.

Biblical References Portraying a Figure Called Sarai

it is reasonable to assume this originally related to a real Goddess perceived as the mother of the Israelites, who bore them.

Klein[11] explains that in light of the assumption that the Book of Lamentations was composed in Israel and not in Babylon, it was not directly influenced by Mesopotamian poetry. The biblical feminine anthropomorphizing of Jerusalem is probably borrowed from Western Semitic literature, through which the Mesopotamian influences were also absorbed.

Further support for the assumption that the description in Chapter 1 originally referred to an ancient Goddess of Israel lamenting her people, or the plight of the city in her absence, is seen in the similarity between the description of the people's experience when they ceased to worship her in Jeremiah 44 and Lamentations Chapter 1. The prophet Jeremiah is generally believed to be the author of Lamentations, so there is great significance in this similarity. In Chapter 44 Jeremiah describes the feelings of the people towards their beloved Goddess, the Queen of Heaven (which, according to the argument presented here, is Asherah):

> "As for the word that thou hast spoken unto us in the name of the LORD, we will not hearken unto thee. But we will certainly perform every word that is gone forth out of our mouth, to offer unto the queen of heaven, and to pour out drink-offerings unto her, as we have done, we and our fathers, our kings and our princes, in the cities of Judah, and in the streets of Jerusalem; for then had we plenty of food, and were well, and saw no evil. But since we let off to offer to the queen of heaven, and to pour out drink-offerings unto her, we have wanted all things, and have been consumed by the sword and by the famine" (Jer 44:16–18).

In these verses Jeremiah reveals the people's strong existential-religious experience of their Goddess, the Queen of Heaven whom they worship. It is she, rather than Yahweh, who is responsible for abundance, security, and goodness. When they cease to worship her, abandoning her and instead worshipping only

---

11. Klein, "Bat-Ṣiyon," 204.

Yahweh, their situation worsens and they suffer. During the worship of the Queen of Heaven, the people report experiencing security and abundance, but under the rule of Yahweh who demanded the separation from the Goddess, the people report experiencing horror and terror.

According to Jeremiah, the people emphasize that during the reign of the Goddess there was plenty of food. "For then we had plenty of bread to eat, we were well-off, and suffered no misfortune" (Jer 44:17). The change to a state of hunger and lack of bread occurred when the Goddess's reign was harmed, despised or trampled and the people had to stop worshiping her. "We have lacked everything, and we have been consumed by the sword and by famine" (44:18). This existential religious situation is very similarly described in Lamentations 1:11. It seems to embody the situation of distress that the people referred to in the Book of Jeremiah reported when the rule of the Goddess and her worship was harmed: "All her inhabitants sigh as they search for bread; they have bartered their treasures for food, to keep themselves alive. See O Lord, and behold, how abject I have become." The lamenting Goddess tells of her parallel situation that is reflected in the condition of her people. When she was in a position of power, she bestowed an abundance of nutrition, but now she is broken, her people are starving, "sighing for bread," crying out for food.

The parallel in these situations reinforces the assumption that the description of lamentation illustrates the people's existential religious feeling of depending on the presence of the mother Goddess for their faith and survival. What is described in Lamentations 1 may not only originate from the nation's grief, the sense of chaos, and the destruction of the temple and the city, but also from the existential emotional violent separation from the mother Goddess, from the nation's life of faith and worship, and the disaster that followed this disconnect and separation. The lament may embody the sense of loss experienced by the people when their mother, who defends them and in whom they trust and depend, is despised and brought low, ultimately causing the destruction of the people.

Biblical References Portraying a Figure Called Sarai

Sarai as a *"meḥôlelet"* in Isaiah

We can also perceive a further reference to Sarai as divine and supernatural when we consider Isaiah and his prophecy. The prophet Isaiah in Chapter 51 calls upon the people: "Look to the rock you were hewn from, to the quarry you were dug from. Look back to Abraham your father, and to Sarah who brought you forth *(teḥôlelkem,* תחוללכם*)*" (Isa 51: 1–2). The prophet reminds the people of their physical and spiritual foundations—the place of their origin, from which they derive their roots. He describes Abraham as the father but he does not describe Sarah as we would have expected from the story of Genesis, as a human mother, or one who has given birth. Instead Isaiah describes Sarah as someone who *is meḥôlelet* (מחוללת).

The interpretive tendency is to relate *meḥôlelet* (מחוללת) *(from teḥôlelkem* תחוללכם*.)* to the verb birthing, describing giving birth in the human sense. But an examination of the places where this phrase appears in the Bible reveals a more unique and special meaning.

The verb *meḥôl* appears in various forms in different places in the Bible in the sense of creation that is not necessarily actually controlled or influenced by humans.[12] For example, in Prov 25:23, it is written: "A north wind produces (*teḥôl*) rain, and whispered words, a glowering face." Deut 32:18 reads "You neglected the Rock that begot you, forgot the God who brought you forth (*meḥôlel*ha)." This is also the case in Ps 90: 2: "Before the mountains came into being, before You brought forth the earth and the world." The use of the various forms of the verb *meḥôl* creates a characteristic, as we can see, of a creative force—a creation and the establishment of a country, people, or nation from the foundations. The *meḥôlel*— the generator or creator is a superhuman force. In Isa 66: 8–9 a similar use can be seen for this verb, which appears in a slightly different form—"Can a land pass through travail in a single day? Or is a nation born all at once? Yet Zion travailed (hala חלה) and

---

12. See Shlomo, "'rūaḥ ṣāfón t ḥōlēl gašem, ufánim niz'āmīm l e šōn sāter," 187, 83e.

29

at once bore her children!" The word חלה (travail) corresponds to ילדה (she bore), but the birth it refers to is a mythical rather than a human birth—Zion, symbolizing a female entity, creates the children of Israel. Clearly Zion is not a human figure but the representation of an exalted and sublime female figure.

In Isa 51:9, the chapter where the prophet refers to Sarai as *meḥôlelet*, he makes a second reference to *meḥôlelet* which is this:

> "Awake, awake, clothe yourself with splendor. O arm of the Lord! Awake as in days of old, as in former ages! It was you that hacked Rahab in pieces, that pierced (*meḥôlelet*) the Serpent. It was you that dried up the sea, the waters of the great deep; that made the abysses of the sea a road the redeemed might walk."

It is impossible to ignore the mythological content of this verse about the powers of the mighty sea, which is also described in various mythologies.[13] It should be noted that in local cultures Rahab and the Dragon are perceived as being under the control of the goddess. The Babylonian goddess Tiamat was associated with the creative powers of the sea, and the cult of the serpent (tannit or taninim also means 'serpent') is also connected with Asherah[14].

The entity the prophet Isaiah calls upon to awaken, (the arm of God) is also called *"meḥôlelet"*—the one from which the serpent was carved, that is, from which the creatures of the sea were created, in the days of creation in ancient times. In Isaiah 51: 17, the same entity that the prophet aspires to awaken is also called Jerusalem. In Isa 52 the prophet again calls upon this entity to awaken, and this time it is called Zion. The prophet's words suggest that the entity has drunk from the cup of God's wrath, in other words, she was punished by Him. If so, then this female entity is a divine

---

13. Uffenheimer identifies the call "Awake, awake" as a cult of arousal of the divine being to action, and as an expression of its power. He argues that the cult of arousal was acceptable in the ancient Near East, but he points out that in the biblical literature the call to awaken is mentioned as a poetic form rather than for a ritual purpose. Uffenheimer, "Awakeners," 163–74.

14. Ackerman, "Queen Mother," 385–401; Buchanan, "Snake Goddess," 1–18.

ancient power ("arm of God"). She is also a separate entity from God since He punishes her. Other names for this ancient creative power are Zion or Jerusalem. If we connect this to what was said earlier regarding the religious tendency in the ancient Near East to call the goddess by the name of the city under her patronage, [15] then it is certainly possible that the appellations of Jerusalem and Zion were attributed in ancient times to the divine spouse, Asherah or, as she was also known according to my argument, Sarai, who was the patron of Jerusalem. This does not necessarily mean, of course, that Isaiah was addressing the Goddess, but his poetic metaphors were in fact terms and concepts that were common in the life and culture of the people.

If we return to the beginning of this chapter, we could sum up by saying that in describing Sarai as *meḥôlelet*, Isaiah is actually revealing an ancient, religious, accepted and popular connection between the image of Sarai and that of an ancient creator, who was regarded as the patron Goddess of the city of Jerusalem. For this reason she was also known by the various names of the city.

Sarai and the *meḥôlelet* in the Book of Proverbs

The Book of Proverbs is another place where the *meḥôlelet* appears in almost the same way as in Isaiah. Here the verb "*meḥôlelet* מחוללת" is used in the first person:

> There was still no deep when I was brought forth *(holalti* חוללתי*)*, no springs rich in water; before the mountains were sunk, before the hills I was born . . . He had not yet made earth and fields, or the world's first clumps of clay, I was there when He set the heavens into place; when He fixed the horizon upon the deep (Prov 8:24, 26–27).

The female entity in these verses, the *meḥôlelet* (מחוללת), describes herself as present with God in the days when the world was not yet created—in the chaotic days when the wind blew over the void, as told in Gen 1.

15. Dobbs-Allsopp, "Syntagma of Bat," 451–70.

The similarity between the way the *meḥôlelet* has been presented in Isaiah and in Proverbs reinforces the assumption that the verb *holalti* or *Teholelhem* was related to a superhuman female being, one who was regarded as Yahweh's consort in creation. The manner in which the verb *meḥôlelet* is applied to *bina*—wisdom—adds to the conclusion that it is a reference to an ancient female divine entity, one who is seen as the consort of God, since research has identified wisdom as the literary incarnation of Asherah, the divine partner.

Scholars have identified the bina as a divine figure and even as the embodiment of the consort of God. Lang[16] describes the entity of wisdom in Chapter 8 as a woman of such high standing that the king himself is said to depend on her. She is infinitely superior, depicted as a goddess who judges the rulers and dwells in the presence of God the creator.

Hadley[17] argues that the Wisdom in the Book of Proverbs reflects the process of eradicating the goddess Asherah from the religion of Israel—from her independent and powerful identity as a separate Goddess, through to her eventual reduction to one of Yahweh's "co-workers," while completely ignoring that she is in fact an Israelite Goddess in her own right. Ackerman[18] also presents the similarity between Wisdom, as a feminine entity called a woman of valor, and Asherah. Ackerman concludes that the tasks of the woman of valor—"She seeketh wool and flax" (Prov 31:10)—are taken from the worship of the goddess, as expressed for example in the verse: "where the women wove coverings for Asherah" (2 Kgs 23:7). In other words, the Wisdom in Proverbs is the reincarnation of the Israelite Goddess as God's consort.

So, if the Wisdom-bina entity is a literary incarnation of the Goddess Asherah, then by designating bina as *meḥôlelet*, when the *meḥôlelet* has been identified by Isaiah as Sarai, we can reinforce the assumption that Sarai is actually Asherah. Indeed, interesting

---

16. Lang, *Wisdom and the Book of Proverbs*, 56–60.
17. Hadley, "From Goddess to Literary Construct," 395–99.
18. Ackerman, "Asherah, the West Semitic Goddess," 1–30.

Biblical References Portraying a Figure Called Sarai

similarities can be noted between the description of the bina entity and the story of Sarai in Genesis.

When Sarai banishes Hagar and demands that Abraham listen and obey her, God orders Abraham to do whatever Sarah tells him. This could be interpreted as a desire for domestic peace, but assuming that God does not function as a mediator in marital affairs, it is reasonable to assume that the verse in which Abraham, the father of the nation, was instructed by God to listen and obey Sarai, attests to great spiritual knowledge and wisdom being attributed to her. Usually, the chosen one is ordered to obey all of God's commands, but here, Abraham, the chosen one, is commanded to listen to all that Sarai says. It would seem that God Himself accepts Sarai's authority. This echoes the words of Wisdom in the book of Proverbs. In Prov 5 we read: "My son, attend unto my wisdom; incline thine ear to my understanding"; (Prov 5:1). The believer is called by God to listen to whatever Wisdom says, just as God ordered Abraham to attend to all that Sarai says, that is, to relate to her words as the words of Wisdom itself. Sarai, therefore, has the distinction of Wisdom.

In addition, Proverbs Chapter 7 reads: "Say unto wisdom: 'Thou art my sister', and call understanding thy kinswoman" (Prov 7:4). This is similar to Abraham's words to Sarah: "Say, I pray thee, thou art my sister" (Gen 12:13). The sister to whom the verse from Genesis refers is Sarai, and in Proverbs the unique description "Thou art my sister" refers to Wisdom (Prov 7:4). Similarly, the verse in Prov 8:3, "Beside the gates, at the entry of the city, at the coming in at the doors, she crieth aloud" echoes the portrayal of Sarai standing at the entrance to the tent during the divine messengers' visit.

Wisdom is sought by kings and princes. "By Me kings reign, and princes decree justice. By Me princes rule, and nobles, even all the judges of the earth" (Prov 8:15–16). This is very similar to the way Sarah is described in the Book of Genesis, as being sought by kings. Proverbs reads: "Riches and honour are with me; yea, enduring riches and righteousness" (8:18), and indeed, it was due to Sarah that Abraham was awarded great riches and honour by the kings with whom she stayed.

Another connection between Sarai and Wisdom can be seen in the emphasis on construction being their purpose. Proverbs emphasizes the connection between Wisdom and building a home. In Hebrew the root of the word wisdom (בינה) and the root of the word building (בנייה) are the same. Built or אֶבָּנֶה 'ebane' in Hebrew is based on the same letters of בינה 'bina' or wisdom). We read, for example: "Wisdom hath built her house" (Prov 9:1) and "Through wisdom is a house built" (Prov 23:3). Genesis quotes Sarai as saying: "It may be that I shall be built up through her" (Gen 16:2) Namely, Sarai is described as aspiring to build her home, just as Wisdom is described as building a home.

It is interesting to note that in the Book of Proverbs, Sarai's name, in various variations, appears time and again as a sacred code name: The word "yeshru" "ישרו" in Hebrew appears in Prov 4:14 and Prov 9:6. The phrases "*Sari*m Yasoru" in Hebrew (princes rule) appears in Prov 8:16. "It will be a cure for your body"—רפאות תהי לשריך (Prov 3:8), "Happy is the man that findeth wisdom" "אשרי אדם מצא חוכמה" (3:13), "He that walketh in his uprightness feareth the LORD"—"הולך בישרו"—(14:2).

"Her children rise up, and call her blessed"—"קמו בניה ויאשרוה" (Prov 31:28), "but he that keepeth the law, happy is he"—"ושומר תורה אשרהו" (29:18), "for happy are they that keep my ways"—'אשרי דרכי ישמרו'(8:32). "Happy is the man that hearkeneth to me"—'אשרי אדם שומע לי' (8:32), and "walk in the way of understanding"—'אשרו בדרך בינה' (9:6)—These are just some of many examples where the letters of Sarai's name appear.

Of particular interest is the frequent use of the word "ashrei" to describe the blessed and fortunate condition of the one who follows the path of wisdom. The root א.ש.ר in Hebrew does not mean blessing or luck (the different declensions of the verb א.ש.ר mean "straight" or "confirm"). Therefore, it would seem that the source of the word "ashrei" in the sense of a beneficial or lucky effect is taken from the noun considered to be a source that bestows blessings, abundance and good fortune.

Biblical References Portraying a Figure Called Sarai

Hebrew nouns can be converted into other parts of sentences. It is possible, then, that the word "ashrei," which appears as a name that means "lucky" originated in the name of the Goddess who, according to believers, bestows the blessing of abundance, fertility and goodness—Asherah or Sarai. If so, the ancient meaning of 'ashrei' could have been he who follows the path of the Goddess Asherah/Sarai will be blessed by the Goddess with goodness, fortune, and plenty.[19]

---

19. My claim that the verb description originates from a goddess's name, or "hides" a Goddess' name within it, is inspired by Wellhausen's claim that Hosea's "anatu ve'ashurahu" plays with the names of the goddesses in disguised form, and in fact they conceal the name of the goddesses. God claims to be replacing the goddesses Asherah and Anat (Wellhausen, *Die kleinen Propheten*, 134). In addition Ball has claimed that Asherah's presence can be seen in Gen 30:13, in the words of Rebecca. Ball assumes that Rebecca's "oshri" remark conceals the name of Asherah or, as argued here, the Hebrew equivalent of Sarai (Ball, "Israel," 188–200).

Chapter 6

The Deir 'Alla Archaeological Discoveries

Evidence of a Goddess Named Sarai?

DEIR 'ALLA IS THE site of an ancient Near Eastern town in Jordan that was excavated by Dutch archaeologists in the 1960s. In 1967, the archaeologists discovered an ink inscription on a wall which told a prophecy of Balaam. The Deir 'Alla discovery in the ruins of a temple date to the 8th century BCE and tell a story from the visions of Bal'am son of Be'or. One can surmise Bal'am son of Be'or to be the same wizard Balaam Ben Be'or who we find in Num 22–24. The inscription found was similar to the biblical story of Balaam, and scholars assume these texts originate from a common source. The inscription apparently describes a Yahwistic cult embedded in the worship of El.

The inscriptions refer to a divine council made up of two groups, one called 'Elim', meaning male gods in Hebrew, and the other called 'Shaddain'. These groups are hinted at in the Bible, for example in Deut 32:17—"They sacrificed to demons (shaddain), not god (Eloha)"

Before the Council Balaam describes his vision wherein the 'Shadain' group appeals to a goddess, whose name begins with the

The Deir 'Alla Archaeological Discoveries

letter 'Š', followed by two illegible letters. She is asked to make the heavens dark and to prevent the rain by sewing up the clouds. The name of the goddess cannot be deciphered with certainty because the letters are blurred and the inscription is damaged. The goddess's name remains uncertain. However, based on the research she has conducted Lutzky[1] claims the name of this Goddess is Shaddai, which was the epithet of Asherah.

Lutzky argues there are two main problems with this inscription. First, there is the mystery of the name of the goddess, whose three-letter name begins with Š. Second, the name of the divinity mentioned in the biblical story of Balaam—Shaddai—does not appear. The logical and likely solution, she argues, is that the missing name is Shaddai, which resolves both problems.

Lutzky explains at length why it is reasonable to assume that Shaddai is the name of Asherah, the divine spouse, and why it is likely that the name of the deity mentioned in Deir 'Alla is Shaddai. However, in light of the argument presented in this present research, that Sarai was the epithet of an ancient female deity, the spouse of Yahweh, I maintain that while this indeed refers to the consort Asherah, it is nevertheless highly possible that the mysterious name of the goddess that appears in the Deir 'Alla inscriptions is not Šaddai but Šarai.

If we examine the properties of the mysterious goddess as revealed in the text, they are:

1. She is essential, apparently the most important goddess of the pantheon.
2. She is the spouse of El, the chief god who oversees the Council of the gods.
3. She is capable of darkening the sky, that is, the heavenly elements—the sun, the moon and the stars, are under her control. She commands them.
4. She can prevent rain from the clouds, that is, she is perceived to be in charge of rain, watering the soil and its fertility.

1. Lutzky, "Shadday," 15–36.

Sarai

When we examine whether Sarai fits the attributes of the mystery goddess depicted in the Deir 'Alla inscription, we see it is a perfect match. First of all Sarai, as the epithet of Asherah, is indeed an essential Goddess. She is the central Goddess, consort to the supreme God of the pantheon. If, in parallel, we examine the image of Sarai in Genesis, in what we claim to be sections of a mythological narrative, then, according to the discourse in Gen 18 in the context of Chapters 12 and 20, Yahweh and Sarai are a married couple. Sarai, then, answers to the characteristics of the spouse of the head of the pantheon.

In light of my earlier discussion that another of her names is "Queen of Heaven," she is perceived as the guardian of the lights of the sky and the astral beings—the sun, the moon and the stars. Therefore, she has the ability to darken the sky, that is, to prevent the light of the sun, moon and the stars, which are under her command.

The ability to cause the rain to fall and saturate the land was perceived in the ancient Near East, as equivalent to the goddess's ability to nurture. In the ancient world rain was regarded as the equivalent of breast milk—both were nourishing life-giving liquids believed to be in the hands of the mother cow-goddess.[2] From this we can conclude that the mystery goddess to whom the Council appealed was perceived as the cow goddess—a nurturing mother nursing her children. With regard to the characteristics of the mother-cow goddess, the Ugaritic goddess was called "the mother of the gods," or the creator of the gods (qonat Elim) that is, the one who created and gave birth to the gods, whereas the Israelite Asherah, according to Day,[3] was perceived in parallel as the mother of the children of Israel.

Furthermore, the pillar images of a female figure with her hands on her breasts that have been found in many sites of ritual worship of Yahweh are part of the cult of Asherah—"dea nutrix" ("the goddess of the breast").

It should be borne in mind that in the findings of Kuntillet Ajrud, alongside the inscription of blessing in the name of Yahweh

---

2. Neumann, *Mother*, 39–55.
3. Day, "Asherah in the Hebrew Bible," 385–408.

and his Asherah, there is a depiction of a cow nursing its calf, the symbol of the cow–goddess. This testifies to the connection between the image of Asherah and that of the nursing cow that symbolizes the ability of the divine entity to nurture the earth and bestow fertility by bringing rain.

Beyond the conclusions that can be drawn from the comparison to the image of Asherah, we can find hints in the story of biblical Sarai that it corresponds to the cow goddess. A point made in the Bible about Sarai is "Sarah should give children suck" (Gen 21:7). This point is intriguing because Sarai had only one son to breastfeed. The point describing Sarah as one who is nursing children is added to the verse which notes "she shall be a mother of nations; kings of people shall be of her" (Gen 17:16). This matches the typical description of the nursing cow–goddess—the bearer of kings and gods. Sarai is represented as the cow-goddess nursing the kings or the followers.

"Sarai" as the epithet of Asherah thus corresponds to the attributes of the mystery goddess in Deir 'Alla, which supports the hypothesis that she may be the goddess mentioned by Balaam in his vision.

Chapter 7

The Motif of the Jealous and Punitive Husband in the Bible

Literary Metaphor or Mythical Source?

IF, AS THIS VOLUME has sought to prove, the name "Sarai" was the ancient epithet of the Hebrew Asherah, and if, mythological fragments about her were included in the biblical story, what are the implications?

If in fact Gen 12, 18 and 20, as initially shown, are actually fragments of a mythological story whose protagonists are Yahweh and Sarai, then one of the central motifs in the Bible, portraying Yahweh as a jealous husband punishing his treacherous wife, may have a different meaning than that hitherto seen.

We can see from the parallel to Ugaritic and Hittite mythology, and in accordance with the Israelite mythological fragments, that in the religion of ancient Israel a narrative was told about the highly charged relationship between Yahweh and His consort. This narrative was likely about sexual dysfunction and the suspicion of sexual betrayal. According to this story Yahweh suspected His spouse of cheating with another god. In His fury He decided to punish her severely and also her children. (In Hittite mythology Elkunirsa commands Baal to lie with Asheratu and kill her

The Motif of the Jealous and Punitive Husband in the Bible

children). If such a narrative indeed existed in the ancient core of Israel's religion, then the motif of the jealous husband who punishes his treacherous wife and her children may have been, at least in the early stages, not just a metaphorical literary motif, but an actual plot. The consort, the Goddess, according to the mythological narrative, was suspected of betrayal, and the husband, Yahweh, envied her and punished her severely, as well as her children who were the children of Israel.

From here it follows that the numerous repetitions in the biblical text concerning the people's betrayal of God, were originally references to the Goddess's infidelity. Overtly, the Hebrew people are unfaithful to God and incur His wrath, but this later version conceals the ancient story of a Goddess betraying her husband. The infidelity is of a sexual nature, and as such it also appears, although in the guise of a literary metaphor, in the words of the Prophets as feminine, with numerous sexual overtones relating to prostitution and infidelity.

When we relate to the metaphor of the spouse's betrayal of her husband-God as real, we can also understand why in Ezekiel 8:3, the deity Asherah, who is found at the entrance to the Temple in Jerusalem is called the "symbol of jealousy." Although the mythical content was blurred and disappeared with time and editing, Asherah was apparently the object of Yahweh's jealousy, and so the "symbol of jealousy" remained, or at times, as in 2 Chronicles, it is just referred to as the "symbol."

In Isa 50:1 the prophet writes: "Thus said the Lord: Where is the bill of divorce of your mother whom I dismissed?" The prophet explicitly refers to the female entity punished by Yahweh as the mother of the children of Israel. The entity previously called Zion or Jerusalem, appears here as the punished mother. This description may be a remnant of the mythological version where the divine mother, Asherah or Sarai as she is known, is driven out by the divine father, Yahweh. This punishment finds expression in the fact that her children—her believers—are forbidden to worship and venerate her. In other words, she is cast out from her integral and legitimate place in the religion of Israel.

Sarai

If we examine the descriptions of the mother as the betraying and cast out in the Books of the Prophets, comparing it with the descriptions of Sarai in Genesis, we will discern many similarities.

The description of the beautiful woman whose name is renowned throughout the nations intertextually echoes the story of Sarai—wherever she goes, her beauty is renowned and kings, like Pharaoh and Avimelech, lust for her. The prophet's portrayal of the whore as a 'ruler', may imply what the prophet Isaiah says: "For thou shalt no more be called the mistress of kingdoms" (Isa , 47:5); and indeed Sarai was blessed as follows: "I will bless her, and she shall be a mother of nations; kings of peoples shall be of her" (Gen 17:16).

Ezekiel echoes God's words: "And thou didst wax exceeding beautiful, and thou wast meet for royal estate. And thy renown went forth among the nations for thy beauty; for it was perfect, through My splendour which I had put upon thee ... But thou didst trust in thy beauty and play the harlot because of thy renown" (Ezekiel 16:14–15). He goes on to say: "Thou hast also played the harlot with the Egyptians, thy neighbors" (Ezekiel 16:26). This description matches the report that beautiful Sarai was taken to the Egyptian palace, i.e. "wast meet for royal estate," and probably "played the harlot" in Pharaoh's bed.

Furthermore, Isaiah declares: "Rejoice, O barren one, you who have borne no child! Shout aloud for joy, you who did not travail! For the children of the wife forlorn shall outnumber the espoused ... For you shall spread out to the right and the left; your offspring shall dispossess nations" (Isa 54:1–3). These verses, like previous descriptions, echo the image of Sarai in Genesis—the woman who is described, first and foremost, as barren. The phrase "Your descendants shall inherit nations," also corresponds to her description in Genesis as "a mother of nations; kings of people shall be of her" (Gen 17:16).

It is possible, then, to see evidence of a similarity between the cheating spouse of Yahweh and the image of Sarai as depicted in Genesis.

Chapter 8

Violent Partnering and Parenting
Yahweh's Relationship with His Consort and His Children

THE REALIZATION THAT THE metaphorical relationship described in the Bible between Yahweh and his spouse may have originally constituted an actual mythological narrative that existed in the early days of Israel, requires a rethinking of the theological implications that arise from it.

According to the biblical descriptions, God's wife/consort was severely beaten by Yahweh. The Book of Lamentations clearly exposes this violent relationship: "She that was great among the nations has become like a widow; the princess among states has become powerless." (Lam 1:1). "Her enemies are now the masters ... because the Lord has afflicted her for her many transgressions; her infants have gone into captivity before the enemy" (Lam 1: 5). The woman who is beaten and bruised, describes her abusive husband: "May it never befall you, all who pass along the road. Look about and see: is there any agony like mine, which was dealt out to me, when the Lord afflicted me on His day of wrath" (Lam 1:12). "From above He sent a fire down into my bones. He spread a net for my feet, He hurled me backwards; He has left me forlorn ..." (Lam 1:13). But it is not only Yahweh's wife/consort who is punished. His jealousy causes Him to also behave cruelly to her children. The ancient Israelite mythical tradition describes Yahweh as an angry husband, jealous of the wife who has betrayed Him with other kings, and who punishes her by harming and abusing her children. He maintains a violent relationship with them, based on wreaking vengeance on their mother-Goddess. He remains with His children—His people, demanding their absolute loyalty and the total abandonment of the mother who betrayed Him. The children's yearning for their mother and their repeated return to her is defined as a sin by God the father, and results in harsh and brutal punishment.

This is how the harsh violence that he inflicts on her children—the people of Israel—is described: "In blazing anger He has cut down all the might of Israel; he has withdrawn His right hand in the presence of the foe; He has ravaged Jacob like flaming fire, consuming all around" (Lam 2: 3). "See O Lord, and behold, to whom You have done this ... Prostrate in the streets lie both young and old. My maidens and youths are fallen by the sword; You slew them on Your day of wrath, You slaughtered without pity" (Lam 2:20–21). In the face of the violence against her children, the mother is forced to plead with her violent and murderous husband: "The Lord is righteous, because He has spoken, so hear all the nations." Thus she tries to save them from His harshness. These moments of servility sometimes turn into moments of reconciliation when the angry husband calms down and offers mercy and consolation. At these times, the disloyal, battered woman is depicted in conciliatory terms that are closer to the "good woman," of Isaiah and Proverbs: "Jerusalem remembered the days of her poverty and misery, all that was precious to her in ancient times ..." (Lam 1:7).

God recalls the ancient times, the early days of their relationship, and the early days of creation. This is similar to the manner in which the *meḥôlelet* is referred to in Isaiah and Proverbs, as God's companion. In other words, this good loyal wife-Goddess is also the "bad" disloyal woman-Goddess whom God and His prophets treat differently depending on her sexual behaviour and loyalty.

Violent Partnering and Parenting

In fact, what the authors and editors of the Bible describe in later stages of the development of Israel's religion as God's jealousy for the pure and holy faith of His people, can also be perceived, in the early beginnings of Israel's faith, as the sexual jealousy of a husband for his wife. The destruction, death, punishment, suffering, and exile of this woman's children (the people), were his revenge on the woman-goddess who was unfaithful to her husband.

But is this only about punishing the people, the symbolic children of the Goddess? If we go back to the assumption that sections of the saga of Abraham and Sarai are remnants of this ancient mythology, and that Sarai was an appellation for that divine wife suspected of betrayal, then we must be mindful that Sarai also had a son of her own, before the formation of the nation. With these insights in mind we must take a fresh look at the biblical story of the Binding of Isaac.

Chapter 9

The Mythological Version of the Binding of Isaac

> And He said: "Take now thy son, thine only son, whom thou lovest, even Isaac, and get thee into the land of Moriah; and offer him there for a burnt-offering upon one of the mountains which I will tell thee of"
>
> (GEN 22:2)

THE BINDING OF ISAAC has been variously interpreted in an attempt to explain why God tells His emissary, Abraham, to kill his son, and why Abraham agrees to do so.[1] No study has hitherto raised

---

1. The hegemonic text does not leave much room for claims that do not justify Abraham's willingness to sacrifice his son for the sake of faith and morality. Perry and Sternberg argue that on the contrary, the binding of Isaac text has a clear narratological focus that does not leave room for interpretations and doubts. Although it omits many details, it is based on a foundation of supreme obedience. Even if there are gaps in the story, they are part of a system designed to eradicate anything that might distract us from its essence. The aim is to isolate attention so that it falls entirely on the story of an admirable father. The narrator makes it clear that all details are marginalized in order to instill in the reader an hierarchy of importance (Perry and Sternberg, "King through Ironic Eyes," 275–322).

The Mythological Version of the Binding of Isaac

the theory that the story of the Binding of Isaac stems from the God Yahweh's desire to punish His consort, the Goddess-mother. However, if, as we have explained, the ancient mythology of Israel included a narrative wherein the supreme God orders His emissary to kill the children of the Goddess because He suspects she has been unfaithful, it is possible that these fragments of the story were integrated into the re-edited story of Abraham and Sarai. In the course of time, as the religion developed, the incentive for killing the child became a test of faith instead of a punishment for the mother. Just as in Hittite mythology, the supreme God-father in His rampant jealousy and wrath, sends His envoy to slaughter the child of the unfaithful spouse.

In the biblical version Sarai is entirely absent from the story of the binding of her son. However, it is interesting to note that if we accept that this plot has a mythological ancient version, that developed through time, then it might illustrate a different degree of maternal involvement in this fundamental patriarchal story.

According to the biblical story, when Abraham raises his knife to carry out God's command that he kill Isaac, a divine voice calls out to stop him and directs him to a ram caught in a thicket. Abraham kills it instead of Isaac.

The appearance of the ram in the thicket seems marginal in itself, in the hegemonic text, but if the story is originally mythological, then it is about the son of the Goddess. The story contains a fragment of a narrative wherein the Goddess is involved in saving her son.

As previously mentioned, the study of ancient Near Eastern iconographic symbols indicates the tremendous significance of the icon of the ibex and the tree. Keel who used an iconographic approach to study the symbolism of the biblical world and ancient Near East, argues there is clear archeological evidence indicating that the image of the Goddess was symbolized by horned animals like an ibex or ram standing next to tree branches or shrubs. Ornan[2] has also presented evidence that in the ancient Near East the Goddess was depicted as standing with rams intertwined with

2. Ornan, "Gods and Symbols," 64–90.

tangled branches emerging from her body. The ibex and the tree signified the adoration of the Goddess. The image of the horned ibex beside the tree and the spiral branches (the equivalent of the "ram caught in the thicket" in Gen 22:13) are, according to Ornan, the most common visual themes in ancient Near Eastern art.

It is therefore apparent that the ram caught in the thicket during the binding of Isaac in the canonical text of Gen 22:13 is not a random occurrence, insignificant in itself, as described by the biblical narrator. It is a powerful symbol in the ancient Near East—the rams intertwined with the spiral tree branches symbolize the Goddess and her protection, and usually appear together with her. Thus the depiction of the ram caught in the thicket may attest to the presence of the Goddess in a very early version of the story of the binding of Isaac. Sarai, the Goddess Ashera, who was symbolized iconographically, as was common in ancient Eastern religions, by the ibex/ram and the tree/thicket, is probably perceived in this story as being involved, maybe through the voice of the angel, in saving her son from being killed.

As we have argued, ancient traditions were first handed down orally, varying according to the listeners, the narrator and place. But central and much-loved themes that were etched in memory and consciousness could not be completely erased. They have therefore undergone processing. The memory of the Goddess involved in saving her son from the Binding was probably well internalized in Israel's memory and popular culture for generations. This could not have been totally eradicated. Therefore, what remains in the edited version is the familiar symbol of the Goddess from ancient times—the ram and the tree/thicket. Eventually the meaning of the icon faded, and the presence of the Goddess was thus removed from a constitutive scene in the Hebrew religion.

Chapter 10

El Shaddai as El Sarai?

"In the vague and unclear period following the time of Ezra and Nehemiah, a period that formed a deep abyss between the ancient culture of the Jewish people and its later culture, which is permeated with the spirit of Torah, there is no doubt that much has been lost from the works of the earlier period. The books that were not in keeping with the spirit of the Torah were unable to cross over the abyss . . ."[1]

THESE WORDS OF THE biblical scholar Cassuto make it clear that the canonical version of the Bible and the Torah is a filtered and censored product. The result of this filtering and censoring is that ancient traditions, narratives and founding myths, and perhaps even the names of beloved deities that characterized the ancient Israelite religion, were erased and lost forever. It is reasonable to assume that the existence of the Goddess, Yahweh's female counterpart, Sarai, was also omitted and lost. The monotheistic and patriarchal censorship and editing has successfully blurred or erased her tradition. The Jewish religion recognizes only one

---

1. Cassuto, *Biblical and Oriental Studies*, 88.

Sarai

God—Yahweh, the Creator, the Holy One Blessed be He, the King of kings, who was never 'contaminated' by a mythological spouse or a marital relationship characterized by paganism and idolatry.

However, I assume that, unlike Cassuto's prediction, the Goddess' name and existence were not lost forever and did not entirely plunge into the abyss. Sarai's name as the name of a Goddess in the religion of Israel, is not mentioned in the Bible, apart from some faint and isolated allusions, such as the *meḥôlelet* of Isaiah and *rabat* in the Book of Lamentations. Nevertheless, it is highly probable that Sarai's name as the name of a Goddess survived, against all odds, despite being hidden from sight. In order to discern it, we must examine the name "El Shaddai," which we know to be one of the names for Yahweh.

El Shaddai appears in the Bible 48 times. Mostly it appears in connection with the blessing of fertility (for example—"Even by the God of thy father, who shall help thee, and by the Almighty (shaddai), who shall bless thee, with blessings of heaven above, blessings of the deep that couch beneath, blessings of the breasts, and of the womb" (Gen 49:25). The appellation "El Shaddai" has been studied extensively, and scholars are divided as to its meaning.

Albright[2] has argued that the word "Shaddai" is derived from the Akkadian word "shadu," which means mountain. God, according to this meaning, was the God of the mountains, where the mountain associatively resembles a breast—shad (שד) in Hebrew.

However, Weippert[3] argued that the word "shad" originates from the Canaanite word "shada." Based on this interpretation, El Shaddai is the God of fields and grain. Another recent suggestion, that of Matthias,[4] attributes the name El Shaddai to a divine Egyptian entity.

Biale[5] believed that the attempt to interpret the word "Shaddai" based on the philological knowledge of the ancient Near East is incorrect, since the biblical editor was not necessarily familiar with

2. Albright, "Names," 173–204, 180.
3. Weippert, "Erwagungen zur Etymologie," 111.
4. Neumann, "(El) Šadday," 244–63.
5. Biale, "God with Breasts," 240–56, 244.

El Shaddai as El Sarai?

ancient Semitic languages. Some of the texts edited by the biblical editor have lost their original meaning, and therefore, the meanings were adapted according to educational and ideological needs.[6]

Based on Weippert and Albright, Biale confirms that the original meaning of El Shaddai may have vanished over time. The events probably occurred at the beginning of the second millennium BC, and the scriptures were written long afterwards. The name Shaddai, probably the name of a divine being in ancient Israel, was abandoned and its original meaning was forgotten, but traces remained both in the edited texts and in the historical and religious memory of the people.

For this reason, Biale is less concerned with the original meaning of "Shaddai," than with ascertaining which meaning or attribute of the divinity the editor attempted to preserve. He points out that the name Shaddai in the Book of Genesis is linked to the blessing of fertility, birth and reproduction. He notes that breasts symbolized femininity with its sacred connotations in the ancient world—the womb through which the blessing of fertility and reproduction is manifested, and the nourishing breasts flowing with milk, symbolizing a benevolent life and divine abundance. By invoking the name El Shaddai, the monotheistic author is basically attributing to God qualities that were more usually attributed to the Goddess in the ancient Near East. By appropriating the capacity of breastfeeding and bestowing abundance, God is portrayed as providing for all His people's needs, without the need for a spouse, a concept which was extremely popular in other religions, and also in the ancient religion of Israel.

Biale attributed a feminine aspect to the name El Shaddai, but Lutzky,[7] as mentioned previously, carries its feminine aspects one step further. Indeed, Lutzky instead of settling for the attribution which was the biblical editor's intention, attempts to identify the deity called Shaddai that has disappeared over time. Lutzky maintains that Shaddai is actually the name of the Goddess Asherah, the divine spouse. Asherah was perceived as the nursing mother

---

6. Biale, "God with Breasts," 242.
7. Lutzky, "Shadday," 15–36; Lutzky, "Ambivalence," 421–25, 421.

of the gods, and therefore her essence was captured in the name "Shaddai" or shad (literally "breast" in Hebrew).

Lutzky claims the name "El Shaddai" did not originally represent one deity, but rather two types of deities. She writes: "In West Semitic pantheons, the commonly found compound names often signified the assimilation of two associated deities who may have shared a temple, and had features in common."[8] She corroborates her assumption, for example, in the conjunction—"Milk-'Ashtart" (Milk (consort of) "Ashtart [Melqart"]), that combines the names of both divine partners. She also maintains that:

> Early Israelite religion offers a pertinent (though disputed) example of such a consort relationship. Documents of a 5th-century BCE Jewish colony in Egypt contain the divine name Anat-Yahu which may signify Anat of belonging to yahu.[9]

Therefore, there is the cultural-religious possibility of a syncretic combination of the two heads of the pantheon, the Goddess and the God, into one united name. Lutzky points out that in some places, such as Gen 49:25, the name "Shaddai" appears in a way that can be referred to as a Canaanite deity with unique functions and blessings distinct from those provided by the deity known as El. A reading of Gen 49:25 suggests Shaddai may be a separate deity responsible for breastfeeding, fertility, and birth: "The God of your father who helps you, and Shaddai who blesses you with blessings of heaven above, blessings of the deep that couches below, blessings of the breast and womb." In the ancient Near East these divine functions were typically associated with the Mother-Goddess.

Lutsky points out that in this verse God the Father is mentioned, but the mother is absent, and in her place appears the appellation "Shaddai." It is possible, therefore, that in the origin of this tradition the Divine Mother appeared with the epithet Shaddai, as Lutsky claims, in the sense of "the one with the breasts."

---

8. Lutzky, "Shadday," 32.
9. Lutzky, "Shadday," 33.

El Shaddai as El Sarai?

If we accept Lutzky's claim, then the name El Shaddai originally represented the two spouses, the heads of the religious pantheon of ancient Israel, the God and Goddess, El and Asherah.

However, there is also another possibility, based on the assumptions and insights presented in this study. That is the possibility that the name "Shaddai" was originally "Sharai."

Technically, the interchange of the letters D ד and R ר are a well-known and widespread phenomenon in the research of the textual criticism of the Bible.[10] The two letters are similar both in the square Hebrew script and in the ancient script[11]. In certain cases we maintain that from a palaeographic point of view there is no difference in ancient inscriptions between ר and ד, depending on the copyist's decision.[12] This flexibility sometimes allows for an interchange in lettering that is not necessarily erroneous, but is a correction inserted for theological reasons.[13] Such an assumed correction appears, for example, in Deut 33:2: "He said, the Lord came from Sinai; He shone upon them from Seir; He appeared from Mount Paran; And approached from Riboth-kodesh, lightning (*esh dat* אשדת) flashing at them from His right." It is possible that "esh dat" was originally "Asherat." In other words, the Lord came with His retinue, with His consort Asherah at His side. The R ר was replaced by D ד, thus facilitating the word "lightning" as accompanying the presence of God.

Shaddai, as noted, was an ancient deity that was forgotten over time. She was in charge of the characteristics of divine female roles. In addition, the name Sarai comes from that same ancient period as the coming into being of Israel, from which comes the name "Shaddai." Given this, and in light of my previous claims, the name of the deity "Sarai" may have been theologically amended to another ancient name—"Shaddai," to remove any doubt as to the

---

10. Tov, *Textual Criticism*, 111, 195.

11. For studies proposing different readings based on the transposition of ד and ר, see for example, Berry, "Textual Notes," 53–54; Vainstub, "Some Points of Contact," 324–34.

12. Lewis, "Divine Fire," 791–803.

13. Tov, *Textual Criticism*, 209.

Sarai

human character of Sarai or Sarah, who appears as Abraham's wife in Genesis.

With the development of the Israelite religion and its emergence as monotheistic-male, the names El and Shaddai—who were originally the divine couple of the ancient religion of Israel—were combined into one syncretic unit—El-Shaddai. This name appears and is perceived as two parts of the name of the one God—Yahweh.

In Exod 6:2–3, Moses essentially erases the name of the Goddess from the name of God. The author explains that God was called "El Shaddai" because the real name of God, Yahweh, had not yet been revealed to the patriarchs. The ancient tradition in which there was a remnant, albeit garbled, of Sarai, the Mother Goddess, was rejected, and the name of the one God, Yahweh, who has no spouse (allegedly) took over in later traditions.

Chapter 11

Has the Name "Sarai" Indicating the Name of the Mother Goddess been Eradicated from the Religion of Israel?

He brought out [the image] of Asherah from the House of the Lord to the Kidron Valley outside Jerusalem, and burned it in the Kidron Valley; he beat it to dust and scattered the dust over the burial ground of the common people. He tore down the cubicles of the male prostitutes in the House of the Lord, at the place where the women wove coverings for Asherah. He brought all the priests from the towns of Judah and defiled the shrines where the priests had been making offerings—from Geba to Beer-sheba. He also demolished the shrines of the gates, which were at the entrance of the gate of Joshua, the city prefect—which were on a person's left at the city gate. The priests of the shrines, however, did not ascend the altar of the Lord in Jerusalem, but they ate the unleavened bread along with their kinsmen. He also defiled Tophet, which is in the Valley of Ben-hinnom, so that no one might consign his son or daughter to the fire of Molech. He did away with the horses that the kings of Judah had dedicated to the sun at the entrance of the House of the Lord, near the chamber of the eunuch Nathan-melech, which was in the precincts. He burned the chariots of the sun. And

Sarai

the king tore down the altars made by the kings of Judah on the roof by the upper chamber of Ahaz, and the altars made by Manasseh in the two courts of the House of the Lord. He removed them quickly from there and scattered their rubble in the Kidron Valley. The king also defiled the shrines facing Jerusalem, to the south of the Mount of the Destroyer, which King Solomon of Israel had built for Ashtoreth, the abomination of the Sidonians, for Chemosh, the abomination of Moab, and for Milcom, the detestable thing of the Ammonites. He shattered their pillars and cut down their sacred posts and covered their sites with human bones. As for the altar in Bethel, the shrine made by Jeroboam son of Nebat who caused Israel to sin—that altar, too, and the shrine as well, he tore down. He burned down the shrine and beat it to dust, and he burned Asherah.

(2 KGS 23:6–15)

THE BIBLICAL WRITERS AND editors fostered for their generations of readers and believers an attitude of alienation toward the mother Goddess of Israel—Asherah. The name of Asherah, her cult and her representation were etched into Israelite and Jewish consciousness as evoking rejection, distance, and a sense of sin, shame and disaster. In contrast, the name "Sarai" is embedded into the religious consciousness of the Jewish people as the beneficent name of the first mother of the people, their root and their foundation. Perhaps because of this, it was so important to delete and obscure any trace that Sarai was the appellation or epithet of the Israelite mother Goddess.

Nevertheless, as the Bible shows, the people insisted on worshiping their divine mother despite warnings and heavy punishments; and from this we learn how much she was loved. We understand the extent to which people regarded her as the source of life—a source of protection, abundance, security and nourishment. Without her, as can be seen in Jeremiah's words (see Jeremiah Chapter 44), they experienced great anxiety, like that of an

Has the Name "Sarai" Indicating the Name of the Mother Goddess

orphaned and neglected child, abandoned by its mother. Despite all the attempts to distance the people from the mother-deity, they still insisted on clinging to her, believing it is not she who brings disaster, but rather the father god, who is enraged and jealous.

The description of the destruction of the cult of Asherah and the burning of figurines of her (2 Kgs Chapter 23) illustrates the terrible calamity that befell the people even before the destruction of the Temple. King Josiah, instructed by Shaphan, destroyed and humiliated the beloved mother-Goddess, defiled her cult, and presumably also tormented, tens of thousands of the people who worshiped her and depended on this benevolent cult.

Ultimately, the destruction of the symbols and worship of the mother Goddess does not save the people. Their destruction coincides precisely with the "repentance" to Yahweh, just as the people foresaw in his words to Jeremiah. Along with the abandonment of the goddess comes disaster and destruction: "However the Lord did not turn away from his awesome wrath which had blazed up against Judah . . ." (2 Kgs 23:26, etc.). In a rage Yahweh attacks his people-children, and enables murderous enemies to destroy them.

We can therefore see that for generations many concerted and determined efforts have been made to obscure, deny, reject, expunge and erase the name, memory and worship of the mother Goddess, Asherah or Sarai, the spouse of Yahweh, from the religion of Israel.

There is no doubt that these efforts succeeded. But still the question arises—Was the eradication of the Goddess from the life of her people complete? Did any trace of her name remain in the religious life and faith of her people?

The Commandment of the Mezuzah Preserving the Memory of Sarai as a Protective Goddess

To this day, one of the hallmarks of the Jewish home is the mezuzah attached to the lintels of the house—most commonly found on the doors of the rooms and the entrance to the house. The mezuzah consists of a parchment with a sacred text housed in a box, on one side of which it is customary to inscribe the name "Shaddai." [1]

The origin of the commandment of the "Mezuzah" is found in the book of Deuteronomy Chapters 6 and 11, and the commandment is tied to the memory of the exodus from Egypt, when the doors of the Israelites were marked with blood before the plague of the firstborn. According to the biblical story this marking protected the Israelite firstborn from death.[2]

The Bible refers to the blood marking as a unique indication of the salvation from Egypt. But ethnographic research suggests that smearing blood on the opening of a house or tent was a custom among nomadic Semitic tribes. Tribes in the Canaanite region used to smear blood on the lintels of the house to deter murderous demonic gods who threatened human life and property. The blood smear was a signal to the destructive deity that the household members had already paid a blood price and should not be harmed. In his study Friedman[3] cites rabbinic stories which recount that it was customary to smear the blood of circumcision on the lintels of the house for protection.

In his research, Aviezer[4] examined the nature of the mezuzah not necessarily as a commandment, as it appears in the biblical text, but as an amulet, that is, an object to which protective mystical power was attributed. He concludes that the perception of the mezuzah as an amulet was dominant and widespread in the religion of Israel. From an examination of post-biblical literature Aviezer concludes that the custom of inscribing the name "Shaddai" on the

---

1. Tzion, *On the History of Mezuza*, 125–31; Yeivin, "*Mezuzah*," 780–82.

2. It is interesting to note the phonological similarity between the Jewish *mezuzah*, whose function is to guard and protect the house, and the Greek *Medusa*, whose name means guardian or protector. In ancient times it was customary to affix a statue or the head of Medusa with her distinctive snake hair to the doors of houses, to tombstones, on walls, and on soldiers' armour— to ward off evil and wickedness. It is possible that the words mezuzah and Medusa, symbolizing ritual/amulet of protection, have the same origin.

3. Friedman, "Blood," 23–28.

4. Hilel, "Status of the Mezuzah," 1–15.

Has the Name "Sarai" Indicating the Name of the Mother Goddess

mezuzah is not recent, but harks back to an ancient, clearly mystical cultic ritual credited with the ability to cast out demons. The name "Shaddai" involved a mystical belief that originated from the ancient customs to write the names of the gods on the lintel to guard and protect the house.

If so, the name "Shaddai" is the name of the deity to whom a benevolent protective ability has been attributed. According to Lutsky, as previously mentioned, Shaddai is another name for Asherah, symbolizing her divine nourishment and protection. The present study supports the claim that this is the mother Goddess, Yahweh's spouse, but adds that Shaddai is merely a distorted form of the name of Asherah, who was originally "Sarai."

In other words, the custom of the mezuzah in ancient times was intended to ensure the protection of the Goddess Sarai over the homes of Israel. Connecting threads can be found between the image of the mother Goddess, in her literary incarnations, and the custom of the mezuzah and the protection of the house of Israel. In Proverbs 8, which according to scholars cites wisdom as the literary incarnation of Asherah, wisdom instructs the people to preserve the custom of the mezuzah at the entrances to their houses and the city gates. By means of this commandment the people sanctify her presence in their lives, and thus she, the mother Goddess, reminds them of her presence and protection.

This is how it is written in chapter 8 verses 32–34: "Now therefore, ye children, hearken unto me; for happy are they that keep my ways . . . Happy is the man that hearkeneth to me, watching daily at my gates, waiting at the posts of my doors (mezuzotay)" (Prov 8:32, 34).

The gates and entrances to homes and to the city were related, in the ancient Near East, to the female body. The Semitic and Akkadian name for female genitalia corresponds to the pubic gate or pubic door—bāb ūri or bābum. There were linguistic and cultural associations between the female organs and descriptions of doors and gates. There were also ritualistic and mystical connections with the patron Goddess of the city who watched over it and protected it according to the faith of the believers. Therefore the clear female context of the mezuzah custom in the symbolic language and ritualistic culture of the ancient Near East, cannot be ignored.

If we continue to trace the connection between the mezuzah, its protective quality, and the mother goddess in the religion of Israel, Jeremiah 44 testifies to the existence of the Queen of Heaven (which, some of the researchers claim is Ashera) as a watchful, protective deity against dangerous and harmful influences.

"For we had plenty to eat, we were well-off, and we suffered no misfortune" (Jer 44:17), the people say to Jeremiah, thus documenting for generations the beneficial qualities of their Goddess.

From this, it can be concluded that the mezuzah was associated with an ancient deity, feminine in nature, to which was attributed a mystical power of protecting homes and driving out hostile forces. Judaism recognized this deity as "Shaddai" but in fact this name is a distortion or an ideological correction of the name "Sarai," which at the beginning of Israel was an appellation of the mother goddess.

Thus, it is possible that in spite of the enormous theological efforts towards eradication, the name of the mother goddess Sarai, Yahweh's spouse, appears today, just as in the past, on the lintel of every Jewish home, assuring its occupants of her benevolent protection.

Sarai's Name is Emblazoned in the Name of Her People—Israel

Given the discussion put forward in this volume, and despite ancient efforts to reject and suppress, there is decisive evidence of the existence of the ancient epithet of the Goddess. If "Shaddai" was originally "Sarai," then the original ancient syncretic combination was not El-shaddai, but El-Sarai. This testimony is embedded in the DNA of the ancient nation who worshiped the Gods El and Sarai in a way that could not be erased. This testimony is the eternal name of the people—Israel.

Indeed, the derivation of the name "Israel" is presented in the Bible in Genesis and Hosea. It is based on the story of Jacob who

Has the Name "Sarai" Indicating the Name of the Mother Goddess

struggled with God: "for thou hast striven with God and with men, and hast prevailed" (Gen , 32:29) or "כִּי-שָׂרִיתָ עִם-אֱלֹהִים וְעִם-אֲנָשִׁים, וַתּוּכָל" (Gen , 32:29), and "In the womb he took his brother by the heel, and by his strength he strove (Sarah) with a godlike being (Hosea 12: 4) "בַּבֶּטֶן, עָקַב אֶת-אָחִיו; וּבְאוֹנוֹ, שָׂרָה אֶת-אֱלֹהִים"

However, scholars, among them Knohl[5] and Kogut[6] deny the feasibility of this explanation for the source of the name. They argue it is unlikely that God would be the predicate and not the subject in the theophoric name. Moreover, it is not logical that the name of the nation should perpetuate a situation in which the deity is defeated.

Given these counter-arguments, it is possible that the monotheistic narrator chose not to expose the true origin of the people's name. To do so could have revealed how the biblical editors had manipulated the original text to suit their ideology. After all, they had systematically erased the presence of the divine consort, reducing the name Sarai from that of a Goddess to Abraham's human spouse. This erased origin may be the combination "El-Sarai," the name of the two patron deities. This combination became, through a typical process for theophoric names (such as El-Yakim> Yakimyahu),[7]—"Israel" (El-Sarai> Israel).

Despite multiple efforts to conceal the source of the ancient name and the divine Goddess, her epithet was embedded in the name of the ancient people for generations, with no possibility of its complete erasure.

---

5. Knohl, *How the Bible*, 222.
6. Kogut, "Midrashic Derivations," 219–35.
7. Sinai, "El Shadday," 40.

Bibliography

Ackerman, Susan. "The Queen Mother and the Cult in Ancient Israel." In *Women in the Hebrew Bible*, edited by A. Bach, 179–95. New York: Routledge, 1999.
———. "'And the Women Knead Dough': the Worship of the Queen of Heaven in Sixth-Century Judah." In *Women in the Hebrew Bible*, edited by Alice Bach, 21–33. New York: Routledge, 1999.
———. "Asherah, the West Semitic Goddess of Spinning and Weaving?" *Journal of Near Eastern Studies* 67.1 (2008) 1–30.
Aharoni, Reuben. "Three Similar Stories in Genesis." *Beit Mikra: Journal for the Study of the Bible and its World* 24 (1979) 213–23.
Ahituv, Shmuel. "Asherah in the Bible and in Hebrew Epigraphic Sources." *Journal for the Study of the Bible* 143.4 (1991) 331–36.
Albright, William. "The Names Shaddai and Abram." *Journal of Biblical Literature* 54 (1935): 173–204.
Avinery, Iddo. "The Position of the Demonstrative Pronoun in Syriac." *Journal of Near Eastern Studies* 34. 2 (1975) 123–27.
Bakon, Yitzhak. "Biblical Dialogues Containing Falsehoods." *Beit Mikra: Journal for the Study of the Bible and its World* 15 (1970) 397–430.
Ball, C. J. "Israel and Babylon." *PSBA* 16 (1894) 188–200.
Berry, George R. "Some Textual Notes on Proverbs." *The American Journal of Semitic Languages and Literatures* 19.1 (1902) 53–54.
Bin-Nun, Yigal. *A Brief History of Yahweh*. Tel Aviv: Resling, 2016.
Biale, David. "The God with Breasts: El Shaddai in the Bible." *History of Religions* 21.3 (1982) 240–56.
Buchanan, Briggs. "A Snake Goddess and Her Companions a Problem in the Iconography of the Early Second Millennium B.C." *Iraq* 33.1 (1971) 1–18.
Cassuto, Moshe David. *Biblical and Oriental Studies: Bible and Ancient Oriental Texts*. Jerusalem: Magnes, 1975.
Coogan, Michael. "Canaanite Origins and Lineage: Reflections on the Religion of Ancient Israel." In *Ancient Israelite Religion: Essays in Honor of Frank Moore Cross*, edited by P. D. Miller et al., 115–25. Philadelphia: Fortress, 1987.

Bibliography

Cornelius, Izak. *The Many Faces of the Goddess*. Gottingen: Vandenhoeck and Ruprecht, 2008.

Cross, Frank Moore. *Canaanite Myth and Hebrew Epic: Essays in the History of the Religion of Israel*. Cambridge, MA: Harvard University Press, 1973.

Day, John. "Asherah in the Hebrew Bible and Northwest Semitic Literature." *Journal of Biblical Literature* 105.3 (1986) 385–408.

———. *Yahweh and the Gods and Goddesses of Canaan*. New York and London: Sheffield Academic, 2002.

Dever, William G. "Iron Age Epigraphic Material from the Area of Khirbet El-Kom." *HUCA* 40.41 (1969–70), 139–74.

———. "Archeology and the Ancient Israelite Cult: How the Khel-Qom and Kuntillet Ajrud Asherah Texts have Changed the Picture." In *Frank Moore Cross, Eretz-Israel: Archaeological, Historical and Geographical Studies*, edited by Baruch A. Levine et al., 9–15. Jerusalem: Israel Exploration Society, 1999.

Dobbs-Allsopp, F. W. "The Syntagma of Bat followed by a Geographical Name in the Hebrew Bible: a Reconsideration of its Meaning and Grammar." *CBQ* 57 (1995) 451–70.

Fitzgerald, A. "The Mythological Background for the Presentation of Jerusalem as a Queen and False Worship as Adultery in the Old Testament." *CBQ* (1975) 403–16.

Fleishman, Joseph. "On the Significance of a Name Change and Circumcision in Genesis 17." *Beit Mikra: Journal for the Study of the Bible and its World* 4 (2001) 310–21.

Friedman, Theodore. "The Blood of the Paschal Sacrifice on the Doorposts." *Beit Mikra: Journal for the Study of the Bible and its World* 1 (1982) 23–28.

Gilula, Mordechai. "To the Lord of Shomron and Astarte." *Yearbook of the Study of Ancient East, Vol. 3*. Jerusalem: Hebrew University, 1979.

Greenstein, E. "From Oral Epic to Written Verse and Some of the Stages in Between." Paper Presented at Annual Meeting of the Society of Biblical Literature, Washington, DC, November 18, 2006.

———. "The Canaanite Pantheon and His Reflection in Ugaritic Writings." In *Ancient Gods: Polytheism in Eretz Israel and Neighboring Countries from the Second Millennium BCE to the Islamic Period*, edited by Menahem Kister et al., 47–64. Jerusalem: Ben-Zvi Institute, 2008.

Hadley, Judith M. "From Goddess to Literary Construct: the Transformation of Asherah into Hokmah." In *Feminist Companion to Reading the Bible: Approaches, Methods and Strategies*, edited by Athalya Brenner and Carole Fontaine, 360–99. Sheffield: Sheffield Academic, 1997.

———. The *Cult* of *Asherah* in *Ancient Israel* and *Judah: Evidence* for a *Hebrew Goddess*. Cambridge: University of Cambridge, 2000.

———. "The Queen of Heaven—Who is She?" In *Prophets and Daniel*, edited by Athalya Brenner, 30–51. New York: Sheffield Academic, 2001.

Hilel, Aviezer. "The Status of the Mezuzah—Between Commandment, to a Amulet." *Maaliyot 19*, Maale Adumim, 1997 (Hebrew) https://asif.co.il/wpfb-file/maalyyot-19-217-237-pdf/

Bibliography

Keel, Othamar and Christoph Uehlinger. *Gods, Goddesses and Images of God in the Ancient Israel*. Minneapolis: Fortress, 1996.

Klein, Jakob. "Bat-Ṣiyon." In *the Book of Lamentations and the "Lamenting Goddess" in Mesopotamian Literature*, 177-207. *Shnaton: An Annual for Biblical and Ancient Near Eastern Studies*. Jerusalem: Mandel Institute for Jewish Studies, 2016.

Kletter, Raz. *The Judean Pillar-Figurines and the Archaeology of Asherah*. Oxford: Hadrian, 1996.

Knohl, Israel. *How the Bible Was Born*. Modin: Zmora-Bitan, 2018.

Koch, Klaus. "Aschera als Himmelskönigin in Jerusalem." *UF* 20 (1988) 97-120.

Kogut, Simcha. "Midrashic Derivations Reading the Transformation of the Names Jacob and Israel According to the Traditional Jewish Exegesis: Semantic and Synthetic Aspects." In *Tehillah le-Moshe: Biblical and Judaic Studies in Honor of Moshe Greenberg*, edited by Mordechai Cogan et al., 219-33. Winona Lake, IN: Eisenbrauns, 1997.

Lang, Bernhard. *Wisdom and the Book of Proverbs: an Israelite Goddess Redefined*. New York: Pilgrim, 1986.

Layton, Scott C. *Archaic Features of Canaanite Personal Names in the Hebrew Bible*. Atlanta: Brill, 1990.

Lewis, Theodore J. "Divine Fire in Deuteronomy 33:2." *Journal of Biblical Literature* 132.4 (2013) 791-803.

Lutzky, Harriet. "Shadday as a Goddess Epithet, *Vetus Testamentum* 48, Fasc. 1 (Jan. 1998) 15-36.

———. "Ambivalence toward Balaam." *Vetus Testamentum* 49.3 (1999) 421-25.

McCarter, P. K. "The Balaam Texts from Deir 'Alla: the First Combination." *BASOR* 239 (1980) 57-58.

Meshel, Zeev, et al. *To the Lord of Teman and Ashera: Inscriptions and Drawings from Kuntillet Ajrud (Horvat Teman) in Sinai*. Jerusalem: Ben Zvi, 2015.

Neumann, Erich. *The Great Mother*. New York: Princeton University Press, 1972.

Neumann, Mathias. "(El) Šadday—a Plea for an Egyptian Derivation of the God and its Name." *Die Welt des Orients* 46.2 (2016) 192-93.

Olyan, Saul M. *Asherah and the Cult of Yahweh in Israel*. Atlanta: Scholars, 1988.

Ornan, Tallay. "Gods and Symbols in Israel in 600-1000 BC." In *Gods of Ancient Times: Polytheism in Israel and its Neighbors*, edited by Kister Menahem et al., 64-90. Jerusalem: Yad Izhak Ben-Zvi, 2008.

Ornan, Tallay, et al. "'The Lord will Roar from Zion' (Amos 1:2): the Lion as a Divine Attribute on a Jerusalem Seal and other Hebrew Glyptic Finds from the Western Wall Plaza Excavations." *'Atiqot* 72 (2012) 1-13.

Peleg, Yitzhak. "Did Pharaoh Touch Sarai? Was the Ancestress of Israel in Danger?" *Beit Mikra: Journal for the Study of the Bible and its World* 162.48 (2002) 64, 54.

Perry, Menachem and Meir Sternberg. "The King through Ironic Eyes: Biblical Narrative and the Literary Reading Process." *Poetics Today* 7.2 (1986) 275-322.

Bibliography

Pope, M. H. *El in the Ugaritic Texts*. Leiden: Brill, 1955.
Rendtorff, Rolf. "The Background of Title ויילע לא in Gen XIV." *Proceedings of the World Congress of Jewish Studies* 4.1 (1965)167-70.
Shaviv, Yehudah. "דע, הנדע, דידע." *Beit Mikra: Journal for the Study of the Bible and its World* 3.22 (1977) 295-99.
Shifra, Shin and Jacob Klein. *In those Distant Days: Anthology of Mesopotamian Literature in Hebrew*. Tel Aviv: Am Oved, 1996.
Shkop, Esther M. "And Sarah Laughed . . ." *Tradition: A Journal of Orthodox Jewish Thought* 31.3 (1997) 42-51.
Shlomo, Sigal. "'rūaḥ ṣāfón t ḥōlēl gašem, ufánim niz'āmīm l e šōn sāter" (Proverbs 25:23) Review/23, *Beit Mikra: [Journal for the Study of the Bible and Its World* 63.3/4 (2005) 268-82.
Sinai, Tur. "El Shadday." *Eretz-Israel: Archaeological, Historical and Geographical Studies* 3 (1954).
Speiser, Ephraim A., et al. "The Wife–Sister Motif in the Patriarchal Narratives." In *Oriental and Biblical Studies' Collected Writings of E. A. Speiser*, 39-48. Philadelphia, PA: University of Pennsylvania Press, 1967.
Sutskover, Talia. "Name Giving in Genesis and Establishing Authority." *Beit Mikra: [Journal for the Study of the Bible and its World* 1.57 (2012) 33-51.
Talshir, Zipora. *Biblical Literature: Introductions and Studies, Vol. II*. Jerusalem: Yizhak Ben-Zvi Press, 2011.
Tov, Emanuel. *The Textual Criticism of the Bible: Introduction*. Jerusalem: Bialik Institute, 1997.
Tzion, Luria Ben. *On the History of the Mezuza, Proceedings of the World Congress of the Jewish Studies/ Volume I, Division A: the Ancient Near East as Related to the People of Israel and Land of Israel; Bible Studies; Archeology* (1973) 125-31.
Uffenheimer, Binyamin. The "Awakeners"—a Cultic Term from the Ancient Near East." *Lěšonénu: A Journal for the Study of the Hebrew Language and Cognate Subjects* 30.3 (1965) 163-74.
Van Dijk-Hemmes, Fokkelien. "Sarai's Exile: a Gender-Motivated Reading of Genesis." In *A Feminist Companion to Genesis*, edited by Athalya Brenner, 129-35. Sheffield: Sheffield Academic, 1997.
Vainstub, Daniel. "Some Points of Contact Between the Biblical Deborah War Traditions and Some Greek Mythologies." *Vetus Testamentum* 61.2 (2011) 196-238.
Weippert, Manfred. "Erwagungen zur Etymologie des Gottesnamens ‚El Shaddaj'." *Zeitschrift der Deutschen Morgenlandischen Gesellschaft* 54 (1935)180-93.
Wellhausen, J. *Die kleinen Propheten*. 3rd ed. Berlin: Reimer, 1898.
Yavin, Tziporah. *Queen Sarai*. Tel Aviv: Resling Pubishing, 2014.
Yedgar, Ariella. "Sarah's Words: the Partnership and Cooperation Between Abraham and Sarah." in *Sound Your Voice: Studies of the Cycle of the Year and the Weekly Torah Portion*, edited by Rachel Keren. Jerusalem: Rubin Mass, 2009.

Bibliography

Yeivin, Shmuel. "*Mezuzah*." *Encyclopedia Mikrait*, Vol. 4, Jerusalem 1970.
Yulzary, Shirley N. "Introduction." In *the Aqhat Epic: An Ancient Narrative Poem From Ugarit*, 9–29. Tel Aviv: Resling, 2015.
Zakovitch, Yair. "The Woman in Biblical Stories: Outline," *Beit Mikra: Journal for the Study of the Bible and Its World*, Booklet 1.

www.ingramcontent.com/pod-product-compliance
Lightning Source LLC
Chambersburg PA
CBHW051706090426
42736CB00013B/2569